One Hundred Middle English Lyrics

One Hundred
Middle English Lyrics

Edited by
Robert D. Stevick

Revised Edition

University of Illinois Press
Urbana and Chicago

Illini Books edition, 1994

© 1964, 1994 by the Board of Trustees of the University of Illinois
Manufactured in the United States of America
P 5 4 3 2

This book is printed on acid-free paper.

Library of Congress Cataloging-in-Publication Data

One hundred Middle English lyrics / edited by Robert D. Stevick. —
Rev. ed., Illini Books ed.
    p.   cm.
    Includes bibliographical references and index.
    ISBN 0-252-06379-1 (paper : acid-free paper)
    1. English poetry—Middle English, 1100–1500. I. Stevick, Robert
David, 1928– . II. Title: 100 Middle English lyrics.
PR1203.054   1994
821'.040801—dc20   93-31813
                                              CIP

CONTENTS

PREFACE

The purpose and editorial procedure of this book are explained in the Introduction. The acknowledgments may be stated briefly. To the editors, grammarians, lexicographers, and teachers whose publications and efforts have been drawn upon in preparing this volume is owed the measure of gratitude understood only by those who have edited centuries-old literary texts. Mr. G. M. Paul assisted with Latin translations. My wife has given encouragement and ever welcome assistance in proofreading.

R. D. S.

PREFACE TO THE REVISED EDITION

Whatever virtues sustained this book nearly thirty years since its first publication will be found unmodified in this edition revised for its newest publisher. Any modifications will be found in corrections and in improved (i. e., better informed) editing and annotation. Because the perspective on short poems in Middle English has lengthened quite considerably in the years since the original edition, the Introduction has also been altered to acknowledge scholarly developments of the thirty years past.

This revised edition is the work of the original editor, together with Eric Dahl, who contributed Section III of the Introduction, "Criticism of Middle English Lyrics," as well as participating in the review and modification of other parts of this book. It found its way to the University of Illinois Press by the grace and guidance of Patricia Hollahan.

R. D. S.
E. C. D.

INTRODUCTION

One Hundred Middle English Lyrics was published first in 1964, and it remains the only students' text of the lyrics that aims at fostering the linguistic competence necessary for understanding the poems in Middle English.

This new edition is intended to improve the book without entirely remaking it. It offers the same selection of Middle English lyrics normalized to the same dialect, and it includes an introduction, conservative glossing, and other fundamental information. Only minor revisions of the form and presentation of the poetic texts have been made. The introduction, on the other hand, is thoroughly revised. It begins with a discussion of the background to the poetry, followed by an account of the rationale and method for regularizing the texts. A third section reviews the more significant critical and scholarly studies of the poetry so that students mastering the linguistic and literary basics in this book will also have a rough map for exploring the accumulation of critical discussions. The morphology, the grammar, and other features of the dialect employed for regularizing the texts are all described in the fourth section of the Introduction; much of it should be familiar information to those who have already studied Chaucer. For those who have not, it offers a reasonable introduction to the language of this edition as well as to that of Chaucer, Gower, and others who wrote in or near London toward the end of the fourteenth century. The final section identifies various formal refinements characteristic of this poetry which are particularly significant for those readers with a good command of Middle English grammar, syntax, and lexicon.

Numerous difficulties impede a full understanding and appreciation of Middle English lyrics. These poems survive in a bewildering array of dialects; they represent wide variations in artistic achievement; they arise from a social and literary context quite different from our own. At least the first of these difficulties can be diminished by the editing and glossing developed for this edition. The others will diminish with reading the poetry together with the history and the criticism of Middle English literature.

I

General Background to the Lyrics   The period of Middle English spanned about fifteen generations, from the early twelfth to the late fifteenth centuries. There is no evidence that before the twelfth century lyric verse in English was part of a living literary tradition: there seems to have been no earlier tradition of writing it, let alone composing it to be fixed and transmitted in written text. It could have had none of the conventions, modes, or masks that were well established by the late sixteenth century, much less those that evolved in the nineteenth century or have been created in the twentieth. In fact, these Middle English poems came to be referred to as "lyrics" only by modern convention, and not because of direct continuity with postmedieval literary works known by that same term. The Elizabethan notion of lyrics as poetry composed to be sung and the modern notion of lyrics as expressing intensely personal emotions can be seriously confusing in this connection and are best dismissed during one's initial approach to the poems presented in this collection.

Although its origins are in part obscure, a literature of English lyric verse had a remarkable and rapid development during the thirteenth to fifteenth centuries. The record of that development is discontinuous and varied—leaving it a fascinating process to explore, whether we can ever truly comprehend it or not. We do know, for example, that many of the earliest lyric poems, witnessed only in surviving fragments and references to them, were the words of popular songs or the sayings of the uneducated, unlettered people. Some of the earliest fragments are quoted in such sources as sermons condemning the behavior that accompanied the songs, mainly dancing. It seems clear that many poems were perpetuated orally rather than in writing. There was, of course, no publication of these texts. However, some other texts apparently were composed in writing and propagated through copies or memorization of written versions. From the beginning these were mostly religious compositions, often didactic or meditative or intended to recollect significant religious events or precepts. Eventually the popular oral verse seems to disappear, and poems of poets, properly so called, remain as the principal texts of which we have record. What evidence there is suggests that the lyric verse of England had origins that are lowly, popular, and nonliterary on the one side, learned and literary on the other, but the records leave more silence than narrative of the early history.

It was once common to contrast the early "popular" poetry with "courtly" lyrics devoted to the subject of *amour courtois*, a poetic conception involving the poet's devotion to a magnificent woman with social status that put her beyond the reach of the poet, a construct once believed to have been invented by Provençal troubadors in the twelfth century. Extensive study of this secular tradition has shown that such poetry was produced at different social levels throughout Europe and in the Islamic world long before the poems of the troubadors. But in England before the twelfth century, "love poems" either didn't get composed or they weren't written often enough to leave any surviving texts. And not until the later fourteenth century was there any significant amount of poetry in English produced at the court, probably because until that time Latin and French were considered superior languages by most of the aristocracy. Though the names of a few earlier English poets are known, none can be plausibly compared to such foreign poets as Guillaume IX of Poitou, Guido Cavalcanti, or Walther von der Vogelweide.

The lack of a strong tradition of secular love poetry in early Middle English has been proposed as one reason for the distinctiveness of religious poetry during the period. In France, for example, the twelfth-century tradition of producing short and elegant songs in adoration of a mistress provided the model for similar lyrics in praise of the Virgin, sometimes sung at contests in her honor. But in England the religious lyric arose apart from this secular tradition, being instead a development within vernacular verse of Latin devotional practice. Rather than expressing the emotional state of an individual, the melodic elegance of the troubadors, or originality in the selection of subject, the English religious lyrics are characteristically unselfconscious devotional expressions based on well-known biblical events and intended to arouse an appropriate spiritual or doctrinal response in all believers. English poems addressed to or celebrating the Virgin become widespread, on the other hand, only after the appearance of Continental love themes in the secular poetry of Chaucer and his contemporaries.

At the latter end of its history, the Middle English lyric form and its influence on later English poetry are difficult to trace. The rise to fashion of self-consciously educated poets, adopting modes, forms, themes, and techniques from foreign literatures and experimenting a great deal, caused the earlier kind of verse to decline. So did the rise of conditions favoring individual authorship, reading, and, hence, fixed texts; the spread of literacy and the introduction of printing were major factors in this. Some continuity can be traced, of course. Themes of spring, love, and death persist, as did conventions of the address, the catalog, and the farewell. Accentual meter, use of rhyme, and a penchant for alliteration continued. Allusion to the Bible is constant. There is an occasional closer resemblance between verses of the successive eras, like that between No. **62** in this collection and I.ix.40 of *The Faerie Queene*. But continuity in English culture and in the structure of the English language does not constitute influence. A literate, self-conscious tradition of educated poets superseded the homely, religious, and unselfconscious tradition of the makers of so much of Middle English lyric verse. In literature, the Renaissance displaced the Middle Ages.

Although there is every reason to believe that much lyric poetry from the era, especially of a nonreligious character, has not survived, several hundred Middle English poems are extant in a variety of sources. Some fragments are found on endpapers of manuscripts or on single loose sheets. One of the earliest texts (**1**) was copied into a twelfth-century chronicle. Another (**23**) is embedded in records of a lawsuit. Some verses are recorded by moralists in their attacks against sinful activities or notions. Other fragments accompany the words for Latin songs, an English phrase being a reminder of the intended melody adapted from a vernacular source. Many poems survive in complete manuscripts, such as three minstrel books and a monk's commonplace book, and in more extensive sources like the Vernon manuscript, MS. Harley 2253, and the Cambridge manuscript. While invaluable in their preservation of this tradition for our own time, the diverse nature of the sources for the lyrics is the reason that the original texts exist in such a difficult array of dialects and also part of the reason that in so many instances it is nearly impossible to determine the date of composition of a poem with any accuracy.

II

The Scope and Purpose of This Edition   Lyric verse in Middle English possesses considerable intrinsic merit in addition to its historical value for the study of English poetry. In its original form, though, it is virtually unreadable by anyone not trained in the remote and shifting forms of the English language during the period of Middle English. A poem was written down in the speech of the writer, reflecting his own pronunciation, grammatical inflections, and lexicon; the spelling was based on the particular system of orthography he had inherited or developed. As a result, almost every manuscript preserving lyric poems from this period differs to some extent in dialect or spelling from all others. (See Appendix, pp. li-lii.)

Then, too, no one during this period troubled to compile a comprehensive collection of lyric verse, so that there is no general anthology that is linguistically uniform. This verse was indifferently preserved when the poems were current, and subsequent preservation was left to chance for four hundred years or more, until interest in these texts developed as part of larger interests, first in the history of the English language, and then in the early literature of England. The few manuscript collections that do survive are local in dialect and limited in scope: no representative and retrospective collection of lyric poems from the latter part of the Middle English period is extant. We have then a collection of texts that are diverse in dialect and irregular in notation, in English of five to seven hundred years ago. Small wonder that most of these texts remain beyond the reach of most modern readers.

For most readers it is no help at all to ignore the problem by printing the texts as they stand, with almost no discussion of the linguistic difficulties, but with a welter of modern glosses imported from various sources, as in the edition by Luria and Hoffman (1965). Furthermore, as W. H. Schofield (1906) put it at the beginning of this century, "in the main, dialect is the least instructive aspect of a Middle English poem that a literary critic can dwell upon" (p. 144).

This seems to leave only two modes of making these poems accessible to students and general readers: either translate the texts into Modern English, or regularize them to some extent in Middle English itself. The first alternative, which is taken by Loomis and Willard (1948), has proved to be unsatisfactory. Translation, especially of lyric verse, is a difficult art at best. It becomes almost impossible when the cultural circumstances from which a poem derives differ more from our own than the language (or the appearance of the language) of the original poem differs from Modern English. Often, for instance, a word has survived with no change in form but with significant change in its meaning or verbal associations, yet one cannot substitute a modern term without doing violence to the delicate and precise verbal complex that constitutes a "good" lyric poem. Besides that, the meter of Middle English lyrics depends to some extent on accentual patterns within words that have shifted, or on the syllabic nature of grammatical inflections that no longer exist (even though spelling may not always reflect their disappearance). Sometimes modernization of spelling and substitution of cognate words is used in translation. This can produce texts in neither Modern nor Middle English, often conveying inadequately the qualities of the original poems, or even distorting them. Finally, no appreciable number of these lyrics have been rendered successfully in Modern English; and the number and quality of the translations that are similar in technique and equal in skill remains insufficient for a representative collection.

The other alternative is to regularize the language. This course for editing Middle English short poems was adopted by an influential collection published early in this century: "The ground covered is so wide as to render three different modes of treating the orthography desirable. Poems written before 1400 are left practically in the spelling of the scribes; those of the fifteenth century are slightly normalised . . . ; those still later are altogether modernised" (Chambers and Sidgwick 1907, p. ix). A more recent edition takes a more eclectic approach. Many spellings are modernized, but where "a modern spelling would disguise an old meaning I have been as inconsistent as a medieval scribe and kept the spelling of the manuscript" (Davies 1963, p. 48).

The present volume regularizes the texts, but its method differs from that of Chambers and Sidgwick, of Davies, and any others. Texts of lyric verse of the thirteenth through the fifteenth centuries are presented here in a single Middle English written dialect: they are normalized as fully as possible to the emerging literary dialect of the London-East Midland region from about 1400, according to the procedures described in section IV of this Introduction. This specific dialect has been selected for historical as well as practical reasons. Historically, it stands near the line of development of Modern Standard English dialects—through Chancery English of the early fifteenth century and the variety selected for printing from the time of Caxton. Practically, it is near enough the "center" of Middle English dialects, systemically considered, to serve as the medium for regularizing verse selected from scattered regions and divergent centuries with a minimum of modification of the language of those texts.

Taken in all, the texts presented here, separately and as a collection, are offered as facts of literary history, although they are not factual in the strict historical sense of being transcripts of extant documents of the period they represent. In this respect they are similar to texts of the works of Malory, Shakespeare, or Milton with Modern English spellings. They are necessary and useful, however, in ways not shared by texts of Early Modern English that appear in the conventions of twentieth-century English orthography. They may even have superior justification in filling a hiatus that is historically conceivable. If there had been a compiler, like the one who left us MS. Digby 86 or MS. Harley 2253, but who had been born about 1380 in the East Midlands; if he had lived in or near London most of his mature years and, while traveling about England in the early decades of the new century, had indulged his fondness for lyric verse, seeking it out, copying, and memorizing poems; if, then, upon returning home he had written out a fair copy and perhaps handed it to "his owne scriveyn, for to wryten newe": this historically credible citizen could have left us a collection that (we may suppose) would not be unlike two-thirds of the present volume. A continuator two generations later, imitating the collection already begun, could have supplied the rest of the poems gathered into this volume.

The selection of poems for this volume is intended to represent the broad tradition of Middle English lyric verse by illustrating its development and principal features from the earliest period from which texts are preserved to the end of the fifteenth century. Most of the poems are anonymous; several are fragmentary; all are pre-Renaissance in character as well as date. As many of the best known poems are included as the aim of representativeness allows, although I have also included some which, because of their length, difficulty, subject, or other reasons, have never become popular. The best collection, in MS. Harley 2253, is represented by **18** and **26–35**, but anyone turning to Brook's edition (1956) of the Harley lyrics will find more poems of high quality. The goal in selecting the poems has been to show the range of forms, conventions, themes, subjects, methods of adaptation, and qualities of execution. In fact, this selection suggests something of the nature of some of the principal collections made during the Middle English period itself. Some additional tags and bits, labeled here "Selected Fragments" (pp. 175-76), typify poems—mostly songs— that have been lost but are known to have existed just because of these fragments. All subjects and formal aspects cannot be fully or equally represented, but at least their diversity and the patterns of recurrence of some are illustrated.

The texts are arranged in broadly chronological order. Other arrangements such as grouping texts as "Amorous," "Secular," "Religious," "Lyrics on Death" tend to draw attention to only one aspect of the poems, distracting attention from other features that may be of equal or greater interest. Chronological arrangement at least avoids this fault, though it is not without difficulties. The date of a manuscript may be somewhat later than that of composition or first currency of a poem; the fact that similar versions of the same poem sometimes occur in different half-centuries exhibits this circumstance in several cases. Thus, the dates given for poems, and their place in the sequence, are only approximations. Some dates could be accurate to within two or three years; others may be accurate only to within fifty.

This collection does not include two elements common in editions of Middle English lyric verse—descriptive and classificatory comments and appreciative remarks. It should be apparent enough to any reader as to an editor that, for example, one particular poem is secular and another religious, or that another poem can be read as either (or both) (**61**). The conventional opening "As I walked through a greenwood one day" has a variety of uses, as do *reverdie* and the formal device of addressing one's lady or lover; the formulaic "I asked X what she meant" recurs; identical lines occur in several separate poems. The most noteworthy element to recur is the request for "thyn ore"—addressed to a sweetheart, a noble lady, the Virgin Mary, God, Christ, and the infant Jesus. These and many more aspects of these poems are sometimes better recorded, sorted out, and evaluated in a reader's notes than in the editor's commentary.

This book purposely withholds interpretations of the poems, even to the point of rejecting all editorial titles for the poems, a feature otherwise common among collections printed prior to this one—not only in the school texts of R. T. Davies or Bruce Dickins and R. M. Wilson but also in the more maturely philological texts of Carleton Brown, Rossell Hope Robbins, and G. L. Brook. Titles set the focus of a reader's attention or expectations, but the original texts did not employ them. Appreciative remarks, explications, critical analyses, and assessments of the poems also have been withheld. It is perhaps enough that the editor has his say in the selection, arrangement, punctuation, and glossing of the texts. On the other hand, section III of this Introduction will suggest routes for exploring the literary critical opinions of several scholars who have studied this poetry in detail.

Editorial help other than normalization of language, selection and arrangement of texts, and glossary is also provided for readers meeting these poems for the first time. For each poem the standard edition on which the normalized text is based has been identified in a footnote, as is the number under which the poem is listed in the Brown and Robbins *Index of Middle English Verse* (1943, 1965). The *Index* and its *Supplement* provide essential information for those who desire a fuller understanding of the sources for the poem. Because the poems collected here have been selected from standard editions, extensive notes and references are not included; on the other hand, these standard editions are listed in a section of the Bibliography. Additional bibliographic help is generally available in Wells's *Manual of the Writings in Middle English, 1050-1400* (1916), with supplements, and in the annual bibliography published in *PMLA*.

"Hard words" that occur infrequently, or words used with specialized meanings, are glossed on the pages where they occur. Words that are less difficult or ones that are more common appear in the Glossary at the end of this volume. Two basic principles have helped shape the glosses: that of avoiding overdetermination of meaning and that of excluding traditional glosses which are patently erroneous or generally dubious.

The printing of carols follows the usual editorial practice of giving the burden only once, at the head of the poem. An exception is made in the case of the first carol (**25**), where the burden is printed after each verse, representing the carol as it would be sung; the integral nature of the burden and verse particularly recommends this. Another (**85**) reprints the burden at the end, for reasons that can readily be inferred.

III

Criticism of Middle English Lyrics   When this collection was prepared in the early 1960s, most of the important textual work already had been completed. The poems had been searched out and meticuously edited so that most of the verse was accessible in its original dialects in editions produced by Carleton Brown, Rossell Hope Robbins, R. L. Greene, G. V. Smithers, G. L. Brook, and Henry Person. Brown and Robbins had also produced *The Index of Middle English Verse* (1943), and by 1965 Robbins and J. L. Cutler completed a supplement to the *Index* which corrected and extended its information. This work enabled such continuing activity in the learned journals as dating, collating, glossing, and emending the texts of the lyrics. In addition, the fundamental philological contributions of these and other editors, lexicographers, literary historians, and bibliographers have provided the foundation for critical interpretation, as well as for editions like the present one designed for students and other nonspecialists.

Scholarly discussion of the Middle English lyrics had an early start in this century with an essay by Sir Edmund Chambers accompanying a collection of the poems published in 1907. Intent on making these generally unknown poems more widely appreciated, Chambers provided a literary historical account of their origins and an appreciation of their artistry as sharing qualities and conventions with early Continental poetic traditions. Critical writing about the lyrics in the first half of this century is found chiefly in the introductions to the other collections listed in the first section of the Bibliography. Carleton Brown (1932) not only discusses the range of manuscripts that preserve secular lyrics but also employs the notion of a "popular tone" in characterizing some of them. For example, Brown differs with Chambers in claiming popular origins for poems like the famous "Somer is i-cumen in" (3). A similarly important early introductory discussion by R. L. Greene (1935) considers the relationship between vernacular religious carols and the Latin hymns known widely in those times from the liturgy.

At least four other books from the early part of this century are of interest in relation to later discussions of the Middle English lyric, even though they were not specifically concerned with that subject. F. J. E. Raby (1927) outlined the development of Christian-Latin poetry from its origins in the middle of the third century during the decline of the classical era to its culmination in the twelfth and thirteenth centuries, which mark both the height of Catholic civilization in the Middle Ages and the beginnings of the Renaissance. The earliest extant lyrics in English coincide with the Latin lyrics produced at the very end of Raby's range of centuries. In a second book, Raby (1934) provides a survey of a similar range for secular Latin poetry.

With a very different focus and style, C. S. Lewis (1936) defined courtly love as a novel concept invented in the troubador poetry of southern France in the eleventh century. It stressed a poet's abject devotion to a virtuous lady of superior status, often already married to a powerful member of the nobility. Service to this lady involved courtesy, patience, prowess, and in some instances, adultery. Outside lyric poetry the notion was developed in the characterization of Lancelot by Chretien de Troyes during the 1170s and in a Latin prose treatise on the subject by Andreas Cappelanus during the early thirteenth century. By reading Lewis's first chapter one gains a clearer understanding of the writings of later scholars that he influenced, notably Peter Dronke, who rejected Lewis's notion that *amour courtois* was the unique source for much English medieval love poetry as well as the root of modern sentiment and cynicism.

Finally, at least the first chapter of *European Literature and the Latin Middle Ages*, by E. R. Curtius (1948), should be read for his plea that all the literatures of medieval Europe be explored as an "intelligible unit" rather than cut into separate national pieces by the "proprietors and boundary guards of the specialties." Curtius emphasized the importance of Latin writings as a frame of reference for medieval literature and learning; he advocated a specific kind of historical approach—not the mere setting of chronological national benchmarks but analysis of the persistence and evolution of various ideas, themes, topoi, and literary forms; and though he opposed philological dismemberment of medieval literature according to national boundaries, he insisted that scholarship in the field would be "helpless without philology. No intuition and 'essence-intuition' can supply the want of it." Whether or not the program of Curtius adequately defines what is necessary today, it proved broadly predictive of the range of options chosen by scholars in this field during the four decades after he wrote.

Much of the criticism produced during the 1950s and early 1960s devoted specifically to Middle English lyric poetry was less than satisfactory, even though some critics were clear about the diversity of dialects, the lack of evidence about genre, the anonymity of texts, and their remoteness from modern ideas about lyric poetry. The Bibliography lists a number of these early efforts and they should be approached with some wariness or even with an intention to identify passages which offer fiction rather than criticism, are hampered by inadequate command of the language of the poems, or make vague pronoucements about the "freshness" or "purity" of various poems. One study in the mid-1960s specifically critiqued a number of these contemporary appraisals of the Middle English lyrics, concluding that scholars had not yet discovered "how to talk about the poems instead of the (anonymous) poets, how to treat the texts as texts rather than as relics merely to be preserved and venerated, how to analyze the structure of expression . . . more deeply than for tropes, rhyme schemes, and metrical feet" (Stevick 1966). These comments have direct bearing on section V of the present Introduction, which develops these earlier ideas about the "structuring of expression."

Among the scholars who published in the late 1960s and in the 1970s, studies by two in particular have commanded attention. The scholarly focus in books by Rosemary Woolf (1968) and Peter Dronke (1965-66) can be distinguished according to the convention of dividing the poetry into two types, secular (Dronke) and religious (Woolf). Part of the success of Woolf's authoritative study, *The English Religious Lyric in the Middle Ages*, derives from its carefully formulated and sensible organization based on three main considerations: chronology, style, and subject matter. While the poems originate in the thirteenth to fifteenth centuries, the discussion of the poems is first separated into just two main divisions based on style. English religious lyrics in the thirteenth and fourteenth centuries are characterized as embodying a distinctive vernacular tradition of meditative verse arising from a Latin devotional movement rather than from an impulse to give religious significance to the refined conventions of secular, courtly poetry. The contrasting style of the fifteenth century does reveal the adoption of courtly conventions—which had a much earlier impact on the religious poetry of the Continent. Of fifteenth-century poetry at its best, Woolf says that "it is far more dramatic, technically accomplished, and severe than the earlier poetry; the lack of the earlier grace and sweetness is compensated for by the skill and dramatic force" (p. 197).

In terms of subject matter, Woolf further divides both of the two main divisions of her survey into chapters based on a set of subject-determined categories such as death, the Passion of Christ, and the Joys of the Virgin. Thus one finds a version of "Whan I see on rode i-done" (**14A, 14B, 15**) discussed among the early Passion poems, which have as a cornerstone the idea that such meditations cause tears in the eye and sweetness in the heart. On the other hand, a version of "O man unkynde" (**92**) is discussed among the later Passion lyrics, which often allude to highly emotive iconographic themes that had evolved in painting, such as the *imago pietatis* (the "image of piety" or "Man of Sorrows" which depicts Christ after the crucifixion displaying his wounds—discussed by Woolf separately in an appendix). Similarly, she discusses "When the turf is thy tour" (**9**) among early lyrics about death and "Farewel, this world!" (**77**) among later treatments of the same subject. Her discussion of later lyrics concerned with the Virgin explores the secular models, literary self-consciousness, and artifices of diction and meter in poems like "I synge of a mayden" (**54**), with its overtones from the secular spring convention and what Woolf defines as its "exquisite imagination" (p. 287). She considers this later lyric tradition to bring about a change in style and language from the earlier examples, which employed a simpler style appropriate to the simplicity of man's emotional response to the Virgin. Even though some early poems of this type *are* based on French secular conventions, as with "As I me rod this endre day" (**33**), one still notices "a sweetness and informality remote from the elaborate artifice of the originals" (p. 137).

The pattern of Woolf's book enables a continuous and detailed exploration of such literary historical considerations as the sources of the poetry in the liturgy and meditational practice of the time; much broader notions such as the general abnegation of individuality among these poets, their persistently didactic purpose, and the clarification that the religious lyrics "are not illustrations of the spiritual man at prayer, but of the natural man, with his love of his family, his fear of death, and his attachment to his possessions, being persuaded and coaxed by the imaginative resources of poetry into a religious disposition" (p. 14). If there is a weakness in the book it is perhaps in its willingness to characterize the finer metrical accomplishments of these poets only briefly and piecemeal, but this is a matter of emphasis rather than incomprehension.

Dronke's two-volume *Medieval Latin and the Rise of European Love-Lyric* is an ambitious attempt to revise established views about secular poetry in the Middle Ages. Dronke especially argues that the central characteristics of "courtly love" did not arise suddenly in the poetry of eleventh-century Languedoc, as suggested by Lewis and others, but instead existed in diverse ages and places. Feelings and conceptions of courtly love are "universally possible" and can be found in "popular as well as in learned or aristocratic love-poetry" (p. 2). He supports this thesis with examples from the Islamic world, as well as from Iceland, Egypt, and elsewhere.

Dronke offers extensive discussion and illustration of medieval Latin traditions of love poetry as they relate to the courtly themes in vernacular lyrics. He also presents a wide-ranging survey of the Latin learning that he considers to be the source for a metaphysical language of love employed by these poets. Here one detects again the influence of C. S. Lewis, but from another of his books, *The Discarded Image* (1964), which attempts to describe the medieval "Model of the Universe." By this Lewis means a synthesis of theology, science, and history within an essentially bookish culture characterized by an intense love of system. Dronke invokes his own version of such a linguistic and philosophical context to support complex interpretations of several passages from the Harley lyrics. In the homely refrain "An hende hap I have i-hent, / I wot from hevene it is me sent" (27) Dronke discovers "one of the profoundest enigmas of *amour courtois*"—the attainment of one's destiny by surrendering it to a lady according to divine plan (p. 122). Similarly, the description in another lyric of the beloved's figure with "apples tuo in parays" (paradise) can be understood as an indication that "they confer immortality on him who possesses them—the garden being both the Hesperian and the Christian *paradisus voluptatis*" (p. 123). Although it is important while reading medieval poetry to familiarize oneself with medieval concepts, it is probably prudent with lines like these to consider the possibility that these poets could also have had completely different rarified concepts in mind, or perhaps only homely ones.

In a later book, *The Medieval Lyric* (1968), Dronke again has a very ambitious goal—to give an introduction to both secular and religious medieval lyrics in the Romance and Germanic languages, which he, like Curtius, regards as being in a unified tradition. After an introductory chapter about the performers and performances of this poetry that is remarkable for its considerable number of historical references to the subject, he discusses the rise of the religious lyric—from its origins in Latin hymnody to the vernacular traditions of the twelfth and thirteenth centuries and beyond. He notes, for example, the new and creative immediacy of image in early English lyrics like "Now goth sonne under wode" (4) which isolates a particular moment that at the same time can be historic and omnitemporal, invoking Calvary and transferring the focus with compassion to the face of Mary. Dronke also mentions the distinctive dramatic compression of the religious lyrics in Middle English and a uniqueness involving light aphoristic touches and a sardonic tone that distinguishes poems like "Whan the turf is thy tour" (9) from the shrill agonies or the horrified fascination found in other European lyrics about mortality. Whether in this sort of poem, in poems about the Virgin, or in more mystical lyrics, Dronke finds that even complex thoughts and images can be managed with "vivid and personal lucidity."

Dronke also discusses the nature of poetry that, in England, predates the more "metaphysical" courtly material. Thus in "Foweles in the frith" (17) he notes its alliteration, gnomic compression, and native diction and explores what he terms its "haunting quality," asking how the poet manages "this strangely powerful effect." He finally proposes an explanation, admitting its subjectivity: "what I feel certain of is that the poet intended the opening and close of his stanza to react on each other and to release associations of unhappy love, . . . not merely to juxtapose familiar phrases so as to fit a sweet tune but to achieve a conjunction that would enrich poetic meaning" (p. 145). Here the usual conceptual frame for the "courtly" poetry is avoided and the emphasis is instead on the combined effects of sense and sound. Dronke thus moves closer to a technical appreciation of the poem for its interplay of syntax and meter.

Like Woolf and Dronke, Douglas Gray is an English scholar who has devoted significant effort to studies of Middle English lyrics. But where Woolf offers a full and authoritative study of the religious lyrics, Gray's book on the subject (1972) seems calculated to be a more accessible introduction for those beginning in the field. His opening chapters discuss the traditions of the Latin liturgy, the features of medieval devotion, and the audience for which the lyrics were intended. Gray then groups a number of the lyrics for discussion according to their focus on key biblical characters and events: those devoted to Jesus and Mary, lyrics about the annunciation and nativity, a large and varied body of poetry concerned with the Passion, and a smaller group of poems on the Resurrection and Assumption. Readers of Gray's book will also become familiar with other important conceptions—for example, the figural tradition, which involves recognizing Christ (and other biblical figures) as revealed by a variety of objects or beings in poetry and other literature, in the visual arts, or in creation more broadly. Thus Christ is represented by an ear of corn, by a nightingale, and by many other traditional figures. Gray also shows an appreciation for the linguistic texture of the lyrics as poetry. He is willing to identify metrically flat lines or the needless weight of aureate diction, but he also argues that devotional purpose was not incompatible with a sense of beauty, suggesting that the craftsmanship demonstrated by many lyrics is related to the visual and spatial splendor of, for example, the cathedrals. In addition to closing chapters on the usefulness of poetry during the Middle Ages for the task of living a Christian life, the book also offers twelve plates illustrating central medieval Christian images and motifs. Gray's later discussion of secular poetry (1986) can be contrasted to Dronke's two books on medieval European lyrics, which cite only a small number of Middle English poems, tending, as we have seen, to amplify the discussion with many learned references from a wide array of material from medieval Latin literature and theology. Gray instead presents a more compact introduction to a larger number of English lyrics with generally excellent glosses and incisive commentary. He also presents examples of political and satirical lyrics, usually neglected by modern critics. In general, Gray's studies combine a determinedly instructional intention with first-class linguistic competence.

Much of the discussion of the lyrics assumes an understanding of medieval religious practice, particularly of the Latin liturgy, meaning the rites and services of the Christian Church in the Middle Ages. A brief account of the liturgy is found in the introduction to a book by Sarah Weber (1969). Unfortunately, her discussion of Middle English religious poetry itself is problematical, relying heavily on idiosyncratic distinctions developed during the course of the book, tending to overgeneralize, and getting caught in circular theological formulations: "Recognizing this gap between the experience of delight and the desire for it which theology defines and the life of the Church bridges, will help us understand why so many medieval religious lyrics are unpoetic and flat. The flat lyrics are those which, seeking delight, use both traditional formulations of theology and traditional forms of poetry in a way that is not itself a source of delight to the beholder" (p. 178). Even so, Weber's account of the liturgy as a re-enactment of sacred history within three main proportions—within the central sacrifice and main communion of the Mass, within the seasonal cycle of nature, and within the Hours of the Divine Office during the cycle of the day—is useful. There are also numerous accounts of the liturgy in studies outside the field of literary criticism; the second chapter of Richard Hoppin's *Medieval Music* (1978), for example, offers an excellent introduction.

Three other literary studies from the 1970s may be mentioned briefly. David Jeffrey (1975) made a special analysis of Franciscan influence on the Middle English lyric. Lyrics first produced in Italy by Franciscans are presented as background to English medieval lyric poetry, followed by an account of the arrival in England of the Franciscans and their activities, particularly preaching in the vernacular. In his fifth chapter Jeffrey presents considerable evidence which indicates that a high proportion of the surviving religious lyrics in Middle English were preserved in Franciscan manuscripts. An altogether different kind of book by Edmund Reiss (1972) provides the kind of close readings of the poetry associated with "New Criticism." Without attempting to synthesize any overarching literary-historical conclusions, Reiss provides line-by-line interpretations for twenty-five lyrics, including eighteen that are found in the present collection. Raymond Oliver's *Poems without Names* (1970) attempts "to define the tradition of the anonymous short poem in Middle English." Its critical mode is essentially definition-classification, with a penchant for grouping poems of very differing quality and topic under section headings such as "Public, Practical, Anonymous" (chapter 2). Its initial discussion of theory and method, with references to J. V. Cunningham, Isabel Hungerland, Marx, Freud, Yeats, and others, brings to mind another scholar's complaint that "many critics, especially American ones, bring with them in an optimistic spirit everything they have learned about lyric poetry" (Howell 1980, p. 619). Such references keep Oliver's discussion of the lyrics lively, but it is hampered at times by the notion that "most of their original meaning is, as a matter of fact, quite explicit and rather simple" (p. 7).

Few of the preoccupations of literary theory have thus far found a meaningful place in the discussion of the Middle English lyric. One essay by Judson Allen (1984) displays both historical-linguistic competence and a familiarity with current critical idiom. Allen explores at length the differences and similarities between modern and medieval lyrics with reference to the allegorical hermeneutics of biblical commentary and to notions of "presence" in the discussion of pronouns by medieval grammarians, with other observations drawn from diverse sources, including modern critical theory. He explains that modern lyric poetry typically requires a reader to decode a text deliberately encoded by the modern poet-maker. Apparently positing the poem with a reciprocal life of its own, Allen claims that the modern lyric enacts the "simultaneous presence to each other, realization of each other, of two ego centers" (p. 200). He distinguishes this kind of poetry from the medieval "clear lyric."

"Now goth sonne under wode" (4) is an example of the latter. According to Allen, it alternates between a third person report of a familiar sunset scene and a first person expression of pity and sympathy for Mary. (More accurately, the latter is an impersonal verb construction with first person pronoun as complement, not subject, and the expression of pity is directed to Mary as addressee—i.e., second person.) This is combined with a conventional pun (tree/cross) in the third line, and the fourth line repeats and enlarges the expression of sympathy. The familiarity of the opening image sets the poem in common experience and the simplicity of the expression of compassion asks the reader to feel it. Where the modern "encoded lyric" involves direct interaction with the complexity of an "other," the medieval lyric "utters the position of a definite but unspecified ego whose position the audience is invited to occupy" (p. 208). In other words, "Now goth sonne under wode" offers us the opportunity of experiencing an anonymous perception of the divine. Similarly, "Somer is i-comen in" (3) is a "clear lyric" that offers one the chance to occupy or enact its celebration of a seasonal change. Even many poems which are difficult for us today were not intended to be so—their conventions being anything but obscure to a medieval audience.

That most medieval lyric poetry is of the "clear" variety is for Allen axiomatic, because "achieved medieval self-hood normally involved subsuming one's particularity under some norm or type of status, condition, or estate, . . . 'private' tended to mean 'deprived,' . . . medieval activities, whether of rule, love, or service, tended to follow pre-written scripts, of which the Rule of St. Benedict and rules of chivalry are obvious examples" (pp. 211-12). Allen also analyzes the medieval "difficult lyric." Such poetry may involve autobiographical significance, as in troubador poetry; or lyric expressions enclosed within third person narratives, as Abelard's set of *planctus* on Old Testament characters;

or those with unconventional use of effects like irony. Even these poems have at their center the "medieval lyric ego" which is intended to be occupied by the hearer or reader who in so doing becomes his or her true self—whether lover, Christian, warrior, or sufferer.

Given their interest in politics, class, and cultural tradition, it might seem surprising that literary theorists have not yet had much to say about the extensive body of Middle English courtly lyrics. However, even the more traditional critics have generally overlooked this connection until recently. Robbins (1980) reminds us that much of what students of Middle English have been reading is court poetry, and that Chaucer, for example, was not just a civil servant but a page and squire to the king, and a brother-in-law of the duke of Lancaster. A number of poets associated, like Chaucer, with royal circles produced some three hundred short court lyrics, mainly formal love poetry praising a mistress and lamenting an unsatsifactory love situation. Robbins offers a succinct account of the origins, development, conventions, and creators of this poetry, especially from the fifteenth century, and considers these poems the most neglected genre in English literature. He concludes that although this poetry "seldom rises above the level of occasional verse," it nevertheless provided models which "fostered the great lyrical production of Wyatt and Surrey and Spenser" (p. 204).

Andrew Howell's (1980) discussion of courtly poetry dwells on an idea stated succinctly earlier by Woolf (1968) and later explored in detail by Allen (1984) and Diehl (1985) that modern notions of lyric poetry are inappropriately applied to medieval lyrics. Howell aims this stricture at criticism concerned with courtly poetry, using as one of his two main examples "Lenten is comen wyth love to toun" (28), arguing that in addition to familiar conventions, the poetry includes nuances of phrase, attitudes that are elusive and multiple, as well as employing delicate irony—all features, by the way, commonly associated with modern lyrics.

A more substantial article by Glending Olson (1984) first stresses the inappropriateness of judging courtly poems according to standards inherited from later poetry as articulated "under the aegis of Brooks and Warren" (p. 228). That is, a modern emphasis on rich imagery, irony, ambiguity, and concrete respresentation is not correctly evaluative of the courtly love lyric. Olson prefers to discuss "certain aspects of late medieval lyric theory which will suggest how these works seem to have been thought of, what kind of cultural and aesthetic context surrounded them, as a first step toward a more sympathetic understanding of the poetics of the tradition." Following an account of the context of performance of the courtly lyrics as songs, Olson summarizes Aristotelian attitudes about poetry available in contemporary adaptations, commentaries, and translations; he explores the explanations of the various lyric types found in the writings of Eustache Deschamps, a disciple of the composer/poet Guillaume de Machaut and a member of the court of Charles V; and notes ideas found in Dante, Chaucer, and other writers. Dante took seriously the relation between the beauty of words and content dictated by supreme love; Chaucer was interested in the connection of goodness and poetry; but the court lyrics often reflect an acceptance of "the possibility of vernacular eloquence without any corresponding concern for the depth or nature of the *sententia*" (p. 244). That is, an eloquent style is not reserved by most court poets only for ideas of significance or important moral statements. While the courtly lyric is related to important literary developments like the intensive and even reverential exploration of sentiment, or the regard for beautiful language composed according to rules of poetic craft, those who wrote or described fixed form lyrics in the Middle Ages generally expressed little interest in their historical or theoretical significance. The poetry was understood as recreation, conversation, personal expression, and music—what Olson refers to as vernacular poetics at leisure. The discussions by Allen and Olson appear in a collection of essays on attitudes and assumptions about poetry in the eleventh through fifteenth centuries. A third essay in the same collection, by Lois Ebin (1984), offers an account of poetics and style in the late Middle Ages, devoting a number of pages to John Lydgate (**65**), and describing subseqent lyric poetry in England to the era of John Skelton (d. 1529).

Douglas Gray has also surveyed this body of English courtly poetry, discussing both the anonymous lyrics and the writings of such known courtly poets as Gower, Lydgate, Hoccleve, Hawes, Barclay, and Skelton. He also considers poetry of the Scottish court and the ballad tradition, though almost nothing of the latter survives in texts from the Middle Ages. As in his other writings, Gray provides generous quotations from his sources, including much interesting poetry otherwise unavailable. He also offers some standard generalizations: that the great mass of minor verse on miscellaneous subjects produced in England during the fifteenth century is of interest only to the specialist, and that many of the later courtly love lyrics are lifeless and flat, nothing but dull compilations of conventional themes and hackneyed phrases. The oppressive sense of sameness results from the limited number of themes which are treated (most notably the formal description of the lady's beauty, the plea for love, the grief of love, and the lover's farewell). But Gray is also a guide to those marvelous occasions when "a rather undistinguised context will be suddenly illuminated by one striking line" or more extended enthusiasms, as in his detection (p. 343) of "the voice of a real poet" in the lyrics of Charles d'Orléans (**66** and **67**), who wrote during his twenty-five years of captivity in England after the battle at Agincourt (1415).

Gray's survey appears in a collection of literary historical essays on the Middle Ages edited by W. F. Bolton (1970). Bolton's first chapter offers an excellent brief introduction to the literary conditions of the era—its poets, their audience and patronage, medieval book-making, education in the era, and the nature of literary form and genre. At the conclusion of his outline of the historical differences one faces in the study of medieval poetry, Bolton insists that "if readers seize on easily available passages . . . and reject those whose form, style or content seems irredeemably remote, they will be engaging in an act of disintegration more serious than all the physical calamities that have befallen the texts of medieval English literature, an act that will make finally impossible any significant assessment or appreciation of this literature, even of its seemingly understandable passages" (p. 27).

In that same collection is Rosemary Woolf's "Later Poetry: The Popular Tradition," which is organized to illustrate a set of traditional terms, French in origin, used to catalogue the fictional situations they conventionally explore. Thus her examples include the *aube* with its song between lovers at dawn; the *chansons de mal mariées* involving the complaint of a young wife or her lover about her old and unbearable husband; the *chanson d'aventur* in which the poet tells of meeting an attractive woman while wandering in the woods or somewhere else remote; the *pastourelle* in which the poet encounters a rustic maiden, such as a milkmaid or shepherdess, whose response is anything but courtly and often comical; the "night visit" involving a poet's plea for admittance at a maiden's window; and the more general situation of a poet praising his lover's beauty and virtue.

Woolf stresses that even though earlier critics are partly correct in reading the Harley lyrics as "a tissue of borrowed formulae" from French poetry, these English poems differ significantly from the French poems which they resemble. There is little analysis of the lover's feelings: tears, sighs, sleeplessness, hopeless desire for an unobtainable lady, or longing for death are never the sole substance of the Harley poems. They are less apt to view love paradoxically or to convey tension and contradiction, and they are not insistently based on the courtly love code. "In the Harley lyrics the possibility of marriage is neither affirmed nor denied. Without any slur therefore upon the virtue of the lady, it is a harmonious and optimistic world, in which, whilst lovers may have to wait, it is the natural law that love wins love and brings happiness" (p. 288).

Woolf then discusses the resemblances of the love lyrics to the religious lyrics, particularly those in praise of the Virgin, as well as noting radical differences. She suggests that poems on Christ's Passion, nativity, and death sometimes resemble the secular lyrics in having speeches isolated from a dramatic scene or presenting self-contained dialogue, but these are superficial similarities. Woolf explains that "in the secular lyric the narrator is an objective character within the poem, and the poem is a performance to which the audience is related almost as is an audience to a play. But in the religious lyric the 'I' character and the reader or hearer must become one; they are therefore more like prayers than poetry and are intended for memorizing or private reading." Speeches are often addressed directly to the reader, who is expected to become a character in the poem, as in the kind of meditation that involves visualizing a scene from the Gospel, and then imagining oneself present within it. This purpose has two effects on style: a strong emphasis on visual detail and the expression of deep but restrained emotion.

Of the book-length studies written by individual authors in

the last decade, one stands out for its range of interest and originality of conception. From its title, *The Medieval European Religious Lyric*, one might expect a new treatment of Rosemary Woolf's subject (1968) with Peter Dronke's international scope, but Patrick Diehl's book is not primarily intended to offer the kind of literary historical survey presented by Woolf or Dronke's study of antecedents in patristic and scholastic writings. Diehl instead offers his study as an *"ars poetica* of (Christian) medieval European religious lyric." While necessarily concerned with historical change in poetry, in the liturgy, and in other religious practice, and also inevitably relying on distinctions of genre, Diehl nevertheless makes his emphasis the form and presentation of content in the religious lyric, not the content itself.

More actively than any of the other works discussed in the present survey, Diehl's introduction meets head-on the problem that "medieval religious lyric challenges not only our sensibilities but our literary methodologies and theories as well" (p. 22). Where Bolton (1984) offered an account of the conditions of composition for Middle English poetry to spell out some of the obvious differences between that era and our own, Diehl considers many of the same historical and cultural differences for more "theoretical" purposes: to articulate the abstract conceptual issues which underlie our preconceptions and to discover an appropriate method of approaching the literature. His initial conclusions about such features of medieval religious poetry as its uniform basis in biblical literature, the significance of limited access to books, or the prevalent role of the poet as a translator (either in language from Latin to the vernacular or in content from the liturgy into utterances outside of formal religious devotion) are unexceptionable, though somewhat complexly stated. One can even imagine scholars like Bolton agreeing with Diehl's account of the drawbacks to some of the modes of interpretation that have grown out of conventional study of the lyric tradition: "The more modern in character the text under discussion (i.e., the denser and darker its imagery, the greater its individuality) turns out to be, the more rewarding is Dronke's approach. That this approach entails the exclusion from consideration of all but the most unmedieval of medieval lyric does not immediately strike the reader"; it has been influential because "its outlook and its selection of texts for analysis flatter our unexamined preconceptions about what poetry ought to be, and its critical approach genuinely, even excitingly illuminates the texts he presents" (p. 25).

Diehl's book is divided into three chapters, each more specific than the previous: the first is concerned with the broad functions of medieval religious lyric in medieval life; the second offers a general account of the genres, forms and structures of this poetry; and the third deals with rhetoric, explored largely in terms of the deployment of traditional rhetorical figures that determine many of the fine details of the poetry. Though the variety of vernacular sources quoted is at times daunting, the overall effect of these chapters is to present an account of the poetics of the medieval religious lyric available nowhere else and calculated to depend in part on medieval patterns of explication. This book includes a good bibiliography of the printed editions of manuscript sources.

As should be apparent even from this brief summary of a selection of the criticism, the Middle English lyrics have proven of interest to a considerable number of critics who have found them comprehensible according to quite divergent critical interests and approaches. A more exacting survey of the main critical bibliographies would show this to be especially the case for a small number of the most popular poems, analyzed in a multiplicity of ways not only in the books described but in many separate articles, sometimes discussing at length the complexities of a single poem. In fact, any one critic may suggest multiple critical requirements for interpretation of any given poem, as in the case of "Myrie it is whil somer ylast" (2). According to David Jeffrey (1975), the poem must be interpreted as having not only natural, proverbial, "metaphysical," and moral reference but theological implications as well—though it is not even mentioned in the most thorough study of the religious lyrics (Woolf 1968).

For anyone new to the lyrics collected in this edition, the initial requirement is not complete familiarity with the sometimes confusing aggregation of criticism related to them. It is instead essential that readers acquire a general command of the language, form, and style of this poetry. These are the subjects emphasized in the remaining sections of this Introduction.

IV

The Language of the Texts   Middle English can hardly be said
to constitute a single language system at all. By the end of the
twelfth century English had differentiated into widely varying regional dialects; by the end of the fourteenth century dialects at
opposite ends of Britain were different enough to make communication difficult.   Until the sixteenth century no one of these
dialects carried enough prestige or offered enough practical value
to be adopted as a standard, or even as a koine. During this time,
however, there was not much need for a single language system,
stable and widespread, because most communication (in English)
was local and because literacy had not yet become common; in
fact, much of the writing that was done then in England was done
in Latin or French. When people did write English, they based
it on the way they spoke it. Besides that, English was changing
rapidly during this middle phase of its recorded history.

The effects are most immediately noticeable in the spelling
found in manuscripts of this era. The original texts of the lyric
verses collected in the present edition embody a generous sam-
pling of the variations in spelling. For example, when the spelling
wh– (as in **whoso[-ever]** or **when** or **whereupon**) was generally
replacing earlier *hw*–, the spellings *quh*– and *hu*– were regional
variants (in Scottish and Kentish), *w*– was another variant (based
on French)—all these representing /hw–/, and there were others.
The opening pair of lines for five poems in this collection, in the
spellings of their manuscript sources, will illustrate:

No. 13.   Wose seye on rode / ihesus is lef-mon
No. 14A. Wenne hic soc on rode idon / ihesus mi leman
No. 14B. Quanne hic se on rode / ihesu mi lemman
No. 15.   Vyen i on þe rode se / Faste nailed to þe tre
No. 16.   Qvanne i zenke onne þe rode / quorupe-one þu stode.

In addition to reflecting differences in pronunciation among
the dialects—and their differences over time—the spellings were
based on conventions that were inconsistent with each other: they
drew from different models for writing French, for writing Latin,
for writing the various dialects of English, or any combination of
these. All this was before the establishment of printing, of course.

For linguists and literary scholars, spelling variations provide evidence about the date and provenance of the manuscript texts, as well as about pronunciation of the various dialects. Skill in interpreting such spellings requires special training beyond that of general readers of English literature. The original documents— the manuscripts written in the thirteenth to the early sixteenth centuries—must remain the only texts on which to base professional or advanced literary study, but they are of extreme linguistic difficulty for anyone just beginning to read English literature written in these centuries preceding the Renaissance. To render these poems readable today for nonspecialists in early English language requires removal of the barrier imposed by these irregular spellings.

The first step involves the adoption of a single written dialect in which to transcribe the verse texts. The present edition uses as its dialectal standard the form of English written in London at about 1400, weighted heavily by the texts of Geoffrey Chaucer (as presented by the principal editions). This does not mean that spelling for these selected lyrics will be consistently phonetic or consistently phonemic, or fully fixed. (This, after all, was not even the case with Chaucer's own poetry.) The consonant /š/ is spelled *sh* when beginning a word, but usually *ssh* medially and finally— *she, shall, fresshe, dissh*. Likewise, /č/ is *ch* initially in a word, *cch* medially—*chere, wrecched*. With a similar lack of uniformity /k/ may be spelled *k* or *c* as in *bak* and *care*—much like Modern English spelling. The long middle vowels—open /ē/ and close /ē/, and open /ō/ and close /ō/—may be specially mentioned. They are the only ones that have retained doubled letters to represent them, and they were the only ones usually represented this way in the English of London and Oxford at the end of the fourteenth century. So in this collection close /ō/ is spelled *oo* only when in a closed syllable, as in *boon* "boon, request"; open /ō/ is spelled without reduplication of the letter as in *bon* "bone." Both open /ē/ and close /ē/ are spelled *ee* only when in final position in a word or when in a closed monosyllable, as in *see* "see" and *feend* "fiend, devil"; otherwise they are mostly spelled *e*, as in *fendes* "devils," *leve(n)* "(to) leave," *wepe(n)* "(to) weep." (Closed syllables are those that terminate in one or more consonants, while open syllables terminate with a vowel or diphthong.)

Deciding upon spelling patterns for an edition like this one is not as simple a matter as these few examples may imply, however. Determining whether a syllable is open or closed, for instance, sometimes depends on meter, sometimes etymon, sometimes spelling. No one of these bases is reliable in all cases. For example, a syllable may be either open or closed according to whether a following (written) -e is interpreted as representing a spoken vowel or not. The language was in the process of losing the unstressed /-ə/ at the end of words; during this process some dialects had alternate forms for many words—with and without this final vowel. The matter isn't reliably settled by trying to follow the patterns of the meter, because of the varieties of metrical patterns that were employed, from accentual meter prevalent in the earlier texts, to foot meter more prominent in the later ones, as well as the shifting mixture of both that inevitably took place. (Section V discusses meter as a formal poetic feature.)

Furthermore, the principles of spelling Middle English must take into account the most common spellings of some of the most common words, when these do not follow the more generally occurring spelling patterns of the dialect. Some words acquire fixed forms independently of the general principles and the ways they developed during the course of three centuries or more. By the rule given above for spelling the long middle vowels, **dōn** would be spelled *doon* and **bē(n)** would be spelled *bee(n)*; yet they are spelled *don* and *be(n)*, and their derivative forms spelled accordingly—*doth, beth*, etc.—as in usual scribal practice. And among the commonest of forms, fixed spellings include the pronouns *thee, me, we*. On the other hand, **ōn** (OE **ān**) is regularly spelled *oon; too* "toe" (OE **tā**) occurs once.

Regularization also includes choosing single spellings for such forms as *awey, than* "then," *hir* "her," *her* "their." Other editorial conventions are also observed for these texts: *u/v* and *i/j* are kept distinct as vowel and consonant letters respectively; any letter not in the alphabet used for Modern English has been transliterated by a symbol that is. The vocalic spellings *i* and *y* will not alternate in any given root morpheme. Further, *i-* is used regularly as the past participial prefix, as in *was i-lad* "was led," *hadde i-broght* "had brought," while *y-* represents the general (and vestigial) verbal prefix, as in *may ner y-wynne* "may never win."

Adopting a single written dialect not only removes spelling variations: it also facilitates regularization of what would otherwise be a wide range of morphological variants. The norms for the inflectional morphology are briefly illustrated next.

A. *Personal Pronouns*

The personal pronouns in this literary dialect are these:

First Person	Singular			Plural
Subjective	I			we
Genitive	my, myn			oure, oures
Objective	me			us
Second Person				
Subjective	thou			ye
Genitive	thy, thyn			youre, youres
Objective	thee			you
Third Person				
Subjective	he	she	it	they
Genitive	his	hir, hires	his	her, heres
Objective	him	hire	it	hem

The alternate forms shown above for the genitive case occur in complementary distribution (that is, where one will occur, the other will not). The second of the paired forms listed (*myn, thyn, hires, oures, youres, heres*) always occurs when it has phrasal stress, as it always does as a complement in a predication, *I wolde that it were myn* (in "absolute" use, as it is sometimes called). The same forms occur when the pronoun is the sole object of a preposition (where it also has the phrasal stress): *And kepe this herte of myn for thyn.* By a separate distribution pattern, unstressed *myn* and *thyn* occur within a noun phrase when the following word begins with a vowel, *I bidde, God, thyn ore*, or with a spelled *h*: *She taketh a staf and breketh myn hed.* Otherwise *my* and *thy* occur: *on my pleying, my lemman, thy pyne, thy tonge.*

Both *myn* and *thyn* will have inflectional -*e* when preceding a plural noun. And occasionally *hir* and *her* will have inflectional (or analogical) -*e*, typically in the earlier texts.

The second person pronouns call for special comment. It was later than the texts in the first part of this collection that a plural form began to be used in circumstances that in the past had always selected a singular form. Use of this "plural of respect," or "politeness," increased steadily during the rest of the period of Middle English, rapidly among the upper social classes, slowly among the lower classes; see the note for **97**.13. Only after the time of Shakespeare and the King James Bible translation (the Authorized Version) did it displace the singular forms altogether in Standard English. The normalizing of these texts to the chosen dialect always retains singular *thou, thy, thee,* and it also replaces the historically plural forms with singular forms when the reference is clearly singular—except (again) when it breaks the rhyme: see **66**.9, where the referent is unquestionably singular, and date is known to be mid-fifteenth century, and the social context to be upper-class society.

B. *Nouns*

By early Middle English the inflectional system of nouns had evolved into a pattern nearly like that of Modern English. There was a noun-plural inflectional morpheme *-es* (as there hadn't been in Old English), and a noun-genitive morpheme, also *-es* (not yet general in Old English). Both of them contrast with the absence of an overt inflection. Here is the normal pattern of noun inflection.

oon	sone	three	sones	his sones	sorwe
oon	flour	three	floures	the floures	savour
his	deeth	her	dethes	dethes	wither-clench

The *-es* inflections were still regularly syllabic.

These are the inflections used most of the time in the normalized texts of this edition. Exceptions will occur whenever rhyme or the meter of a line requires retaining an alternate form. These are of two main kinds. One of the not uncommon noun-plural inflections (especially in southern dialects) was *-en* (its only survival in Modern English occurs in *oxen*). While Chaucer, say, may have regularly written *woundes*, he would readily have understood *wounden*, even as he regularly pluralized *eye* as *eyen*, and

xxxviii

similarly several other words as well. The other alternate forms involve survival of older plurals, chiefly in the most everyday of words. *Thyng* is the most frequent of these; identical singular and plural forms sometimes give exact rhyme (see **33**.4, 6), or plural *thyng* will rhyme with infinitive *synge* (as **42**.7–8). The plural of *hond* occurs variously in Middle English as *honde, hondes, honden, hend(e)*. With *honde*, but not with *honden* or *hondes*, the final syllable can be elided before certain following words, if meter calls for it. Similar to the singular and plural *thyng* are identical nominative and possessive singular forms of *lady* and *hevene*.

Occasionally (again chiefly in the earlier texts) there is another vestige of case inflection that no longer survives in English. It is essentially a "prepositional case," remaining in a few phrases that must have been formulaic—having survived intact as collocations, with an archaic case inflection preserved with the noun. Thus *wyth childe* (**10**.12), *in boure* (**29**.1), *to grounde* (**35**.6).

And a few double forms occur, such as *wyl, wylle*; usually these forms continue double forms that had occurred in Old English.

C. *Adjectives*

Generally, monosyllabic adjective stems, the possessive pronouns *myn, thyn,* and a few others, appear with the following inflectional pattern:

$$
\begin{array}{r}
\text{a} \quad \text{good man} \\
\text{the / that / thy} \quad \text{gode man} \\
\text{Come,} \quad \text{gode man, . . .} \\
\text{(the / tho / . . .)} \quad \text{gode men}
\end{array}
$$

thyn hond	al my lyf	swich a dede
thyne hondes	alle her lyves	swiche dedes

Comparison of adjectives is similar to that in Modern English, with suffixed comparative morphemes *-er, -est,* or phrasal construction with *more* or *most*. Any adjectives with alternate stem forms (called "morphophonemic alternation"), such as *swete, swetter, swettest* will have their forms listed in the Glossary.

D. *Verbs*

The morphology of verbs for this collection is represented by two paradigms. *Stele(n)* "(to) steal" exemplifies "strong" verbs (others are *synge(n)*, *bere(n)*, *breke(n)*); these mark past tense and passive (or past) participle by alternation of the stem vowel. *Love(n)* exemplifies "weak" verbs, which mark past tense and passive participle with a suffix containing a dental stop consonant ([d] or [t]).

stele(n)	love(n)	*Infinitive*
stelyng	lovyng	*Present participle*
stolen	loved	*Passive participle*
stel	love	*Imperative singular*
steleth, stele	loveth, love	*Imperative plural*

The finite forms are as follows:

Present Indicative

(I)	stele	love	(we)	stele(n)	love(n)
(thou)	stelest	lovest	(ye)	stele(n)	love(n)
(he, etc.)	steleth	loveth	(they)	stele(n)	love(n)

Subjunctive

Sing.	stele	love	*Pl.*	stele(n)	love(n)

Past Indicative

(I)	stal	lovede	(we)	stele(n)	lovede(n)
(thou)	stele	lovedest	(ye)	stele(n)	lovede(n)
(he)	stal	lovede	(they)	stele(n)	lovede(n)

Subjunctive

Sing.	stele	lovede	*Pl.*	stele(n)	lovede(n)

E. *Adverbs, prepositions, particles, demonstratives, interjections*

These forms, if not similar to those of Modern English, are listed in the Glossary. Only two small points will be mentioned. Forms of the "demonstratives" in Middle English are different from those of Modern English: *that–tho, this–thise* (*tho* is always a plural demonstrative). And while adverbs may have an *-ly* suffix, as in Modern English, a number of them have instead the suffix *-e*.

Next, the phonology of the dialect represented in this edition. The consonants are these:

Phonemic Symbol	Middle English Spellings	As in Modern English
/p/	pere, hap	*peer*
/b/	bere, but	*bear*
/t/	tere, it	*tear*
/d/	dere, bed	*dear*
/k/	kyn, care, quene, pak, six	*kin*
/g/	gon, agulte	*go*
/m/	mele, am	*meal*
/n/	nere, an, signe	*near*
/l/	litel, lere	*little*
/r/	rede, bour	*rear*
/w/	were, sorwe	*were*
/y/	yeelde, ayeins	*yield*
/h/	here, herte	*hear*
/s/	so, certain, aske, lesse, six	*so*
/z/	rose, lese	*rose*
/f/	fere, staff	*staff*
/v/	vale, staves	*vale, staves*
/θ/	ther, lieth	*thin*
/ð/	blithe, other	*blithe*
/x/	soghte, thoght, thogh	------*
/č/	chere, wrecched	*cheer*
/ǰ/	daunger, juggement	*judge*
/š/	sholde, fresshe	*should*

*As in German **machen**, Johann Sebastian **Bach**.

Phoneme	Spelling	Pronounced	as in	The Modern English	as in	Cognate is
/ī/	i, y	[iː]	side, wyf	[aɪ]		side, wife
/i/	i, y	[ɪ]	drynke, bidde	[ɪ]		drink, bid
/ē/	e, ee	[eː]	swete, feet	[i]		sweet, feet
/ē/	e, ee	[ɛː]	lede, seed	[i]		lead, seed
/e/	e	[ɛ]	helpe	[ɛ]		help
/ā/	a	[aː]	name, cas	[e]		name, case
/a/	a	[a]	can	[æ]		can
/ō/	o, oo	[oː]	fode, mood	[u]		food, mood
/ō/	o, oo	[ɔː]	bon, soule	[o]		bone, soul
/o/	o	[ɔ]	oxe	[a]		ox
/ū/	ou, ow	[uː]	hous	[aʊ]		house
/u/	u, o	[ʊ]	under, sone	[ʌ]		under, son
/ay/	ai, ay, ei, ey	[æɪ]	day, pleye	[e] or [eɪ]		day, play
/oy/	oi, oy	[ɔɪ]	boy, vois	[ɔɪ]		boy, voice
/iw/	u, eu, ew	[ɪʊ] or [ɛʊ]	pure, dewe	[ɪu, ju] or [u]		pure, dew
/aw/	o, ou, ow	[ɔʊ] or [aʊ]	thoght, taughte,	[ɔ]		thought, taught,
	au, aw		saw			saw

[ə], as in **attack** [əˈtæk], is the neutral unstressed vowel.

The vowels and diphthongs are shown on the page opposite. The diphthongs /ay iw aw oy/ are all 'falling'—that is, the onset (the sound with which it begins) carries the stress or syllable beat, and the following off-glide (as the stress fades) is toward a target point that is another part of the overall vocalic "grid." Phonetic notation represents the onset vowel and the target with two symbols. The first three of these diphthongs evolved from Old English, and accommodated borrowings from both Anglo-Danish and Anglo-French. The fourth one was incorporated into the vocalic system as a result of borrowing a number of French words with a similar diphthong.

Word stress has changed little in the history of English. It will seldom be different in these texts from what it would be in Modern English except in the instance of some French words newly borrowed into English, chiefly in the fourteenth century: in these instances the metrical pattern will nearly always make the stress pattern clear—see for example the rhymes in **85**.

The Middle English lexicon differs more from Modern English than is often realized, when so many of the words (especially as spelled here, or in Chaucer's texts, or even Malory's) are recognizable cognates with Modern English words. The Glossary, as well as the glosses on the pages of texts, should be regarded as quite minimal information about the lexicon, particularly the meanings of words. The best reference for additional lexical information is the *Middle English Dictionary.*

Punctuation, which pertains to written texts rather than to language, is entirely editorial in these texts, and is based on the conventions of standard Modern English. By comparison with the pointing of the handwritten original texts, the punctuation given here is much more detailed and specific ("fussy" may describe it better), just as in all modern editions of this poetry.

At this point something should be said about the relations between normalization and emendation of texts, as these occur in the process of transcribing (or translating) texts into the incipient literary dialect. Normalization entails (1) reshaping morphemes of a text in one dialect to conform to the usual shape of the corresponding morphemes in another and, for some inflections, choosing the expected allomorphs of the target dialect over any others that may occur in the original one; and (2) adopting a stable spelling practice, i.e., settling on a single spelling for any morpheme. That is a technical way to describe the process. Less formally, it means, for example, replacing "When þe nyhtegale singes" with "Whan the nyghtengale syngeth" (**32**.1). The lexemes remain the same, and the meter of the phrase does not change. Such changes are always made unless they would cause some prosodic element (such as rhyme) to fail (see **31**.60, for example).

Emendation, by contrast, entails addition, deletion, or substitution in the sequence of the morphemes of a text, or the reordering of them. "Nou y may ȝef y wole" is altered to "Now I may if that you leste" (**33**.23). Emendation is undertaken as primarily a textual or critical procedure to correct an obvious error in the original text, or to restore a rhyme, or to regularize a line, or to improve the sense—when careless transcription is suspected. Most emendations in this collection are minor adjustments to texts; several are modeled on readings in other copies or versions of a poem; nearly all of them have been suggested by previous editors. (Among the changes introduced in this collection are those for **32**.18, **33**.23, and **39**.12 (*weild*).) One text (**19**) has been virtually dismantled and reassembled. Except for established restorations and corrections in standard editions, and for a few regular replacements—such as *but* for *ac*, *wyth* for *mid*—emendations are recorded in the footnotes.

Normalization of the spelling and the linguistic morphology does not change the words and it affects very little the basis for recognizing the meter. Here is a thirteenth-century text, followed by a normalized version (**24**):

> Murie a tyme I telle in May
>   Wan bricte blosmen brekeþ on tre;
> Þeise foules singe nyt ant day:
>   In ilche grene is gamen an gle.

> Myrie a tyme I telle in May
>   Whan brighte blosmes breken on tree;
> Thise foweles syngen nyght and day:
>   In ilke grene is gamen and glee.

Both versions have the same sequence of morphemes—whether word stems or grammatical inflections—and they can be read with the same number of syllables, which are in the same metrical pattern because they are arranged according to identical patterns of word stress and phrasal structure.

V

Some Features of Form and Style   Like its language, the meter of Middle English verse can hardly be thought of as a single system, whether of verse-line structure or of larger forms of whatever kind. The language was diverse and rapidly changing, and so was the meter, particularly that used for lyric verse.

The meter of the texts that survive is virtually all stanzaic, or stanzalike, as noted earlier.   But what is remarkable is the thoroughness of the canvassing of stanza forms.   The simplest forms are pairs of rhymed couplets, *aabb* (**1, 4**), or alternating rhymes *abab* (**23, 24**)—or most unusually a set of four lines with the same rhyme *aaaa* (**26**). Still another pattern is *abcb* (**56**).

Any of these, of course, may be repeated as simply the four-line stanza pattern for a poem of any length (such as **32** or **87**). And any of these, in turn, may be linked by a repeating final line for each stanza, such as *aaay bbby*, etc. (**57, 80, 91, 95, 98**, for example). Then there are virtuoso performances in which one of the rhymes is retained through the series of stanzas making up the poem, further linking the four-line clusters (**100** is the best). Or even more constraining is the repetition of *aaab* throughout all five stanzas of a poem (**96**). In all these varieties, though, the stanza pattern itself remains rather simple.

Rhyme to join lines in successive pairs without forming stanzas also retains a radical simplicity of form. This metrical pattern does not occur very often in the lyric verse (**6, 9, 21**, and **99**); on the other hand it is a staple of Middle English romances and other narratives in verse.

The more complex stanza forms are many and need not be fully catalogued here.   They range from linking lines in groups of six (**18, 19, 39, 42**), or eight (**34-35, 50-51, 97**, and others), or ten (**5, 31**, et al.), or twelve lines (**28, 43**), to linking them in odd numbers of lines—five (**68, 85**, for instance) or seven (**2, 75**, and more), or nine (**11, 86**). And then there are French forms of fixed length and rhyme scheme, with a repeating line (**66, 67,**

71). For some it is hard to tell just what lengths of text should be separated and counted as lines (**3, 25, 30, 38, 82**).

In considering meter in Middle English verse, it is useful to spell out what rhyme consists of. In simplest terms, it is a particular kind of recurrence of speech material—typically, the recurrence of a stressed vowel and any succeeding consonants in the same syllable: *see–thee–tree–be, stour–flour–tour–honour, born–thorn–forlorn, broght–soght–thoght–wroght,* and so on. Although most rhymes are "perfect" (i.e., incorporating the same phonemes), it is not unusual to find "near" rhymes, which employ recurrence of phonemes of the same phonological class: *bithoghte–ofte* (**6**.1-2), *rynde–longynge* (**56**.18, 20 and 26, 28), or others (see **33**).

But also typically in Middle English (unlike Modern English language and meter) the rhyme recurrence may entail a following unstressed syllable, so that two-syllable rhymes *telle–dwelle, space–grace–face, herte–smerte, mynde–kynde–fynde* and the like are unexceptionable. This is a specially interesting aspect of the meter, because it is so fundamentally a function of the structures of words in Middle English. At the beginning of this stage in the evolution of the language there were remnants of an earlier, elaborate system of grammatical case inflections of nouns and adjectives and various inflections of verbs. Most of these inflections (such as *-ed, -es, eth, -en*) were separate syllables, and so was the general, vestigial *-e* inflection. Thus, *Whan I thenke thynges three* has seven syllables, *The riche ladies in her bour* has eight. (In these instances any "extra" syllable is not found in a rhyme word.) Moreover, the position of rhyme words, which is always at the end of a verse line, almost without exception coincided at this time with the end of a syntactic pattern; if the line does not call for end punctuation (by modern convention), its end at least coincides with the end of a noun phrase, a modifying phrase, a clause, or the like. In short, run-on lines were not ordinarily employed in this tradition. By the end of Middle English, most of the final unstressed *-e* inflections had been lost in speech, and the rhyme still held. At this time, despite the difference in the spelled forms in rhymes, the difference between *blast* and *faste* or between *space* and *cas* would have disappeared; in the transition, the difference was probably not considered to be a flaw in the meter.

Rhyme links lines to form stanzas, and sometimes it also links stanzas together. Division of lines into stanzas accordingly is marked by the juncture of two (repeating) rhyme patterns (e.g., *abab cdcd*). Almost without exception the division occurs at a sentence boundary in Middle English (which is the juncture of two sentence patterns). And division normally coincides with juncture of paragraph-like units of discourse (such as in **43**). It is this patterning of larger units, rather than the rhyme scheme, for instance, that groups lines in fours in **87**. The larger units are marked variously—by change of speaker (**89**), by recurrence of address-and-response sequence (**19**), by recurrence of a line (**88**), or other factors.

The word stock rapidly took on new traits during this period, and this too had an effect on the meter. Several of the earliest texts are made up entirely of words native to English: if half a handful of words such as *wrong* (from Anglo-Danish) and the bird-cry *cuckoo* (from Anglo-French) are excepted, texts **1-9** draw entirely on the native English vocabulary. In **10** *grace* and *fruit* are "new," from Anglo-French. In **49-50** quite a number of nouns, adjectives, and verbs are French-derived, and several of them are used for rhyme. In **75** most of the rhyme words are from French.

With the incorporation into English of more and more words from Anglo-French, especially in the latter fourteenth and early fifteenth centuries, the accommodation of meter and word structure took on still another characteristic: rhymes with two syllables, the *second* one being stressed, begin to occur fairly commonly, such as *resóun–tresóun–sesóun*. And when words retain the stress pattern of French from which they were recently borrowed, *gardyn* will rhyme with *wyne–dyne–thyn*. In addition, a number of native English words were being displaced by borrowings from French.

The other fundamental element of English meter is the smallest unit to recur within a line in a regular and patterned way. This basic unit is usually called a "foot," and from that terminology more confusion than clarity has come about. The reason is that the study of prosody in English has focused on poetry subsequent to Middle English, not to mention taking French or Latin or classical Greek formulations as models—and sources of terminology—for trying to understand English meter. The best way to understand this minimal recurring unit of Middle English meter is to learn first the structure of words in Old English and the prosody of its verse (which counted stress accents, not the syllables in "feet") and then study the stages of its transition during Middle English. Failing that, the next best way is to pay attention to the *linguistic* prosodic patterns of the language, the natural segmentation of sentences into phrases, and the prominent syllables within those phrases. These patterns have changed so little from Middle to Modern English that these smallest elements of the meter and the patterns they form are not very difficult to recognize and bring into any reading of the texts.

If for much of the early Middle English verse we can set aside the term "foot," it will also be easier to put aside other metrical terms customarily associated with it as well—iamb, trochee, anapest, or whatever. And without those terms, the meter of a line or a text cannot be described as, say, mostly iambic, but with occasional substitution of trochaic feet. To describe the meter of these texts in these terms is to assume that the units of composition in Middle English regularly were "feet" of these types; "substitution," "replacement," and terms like these have no meaning in discussing meter unless the assumption of foot meter is right. That assumption appears to have been wrong, despite its long life and lingering effects.

The established notion of "foot" is built upon patterns of syllables. Meter can have syllable patterns as the smallest regular and recurring unit, of course, as texts in Latin, Modern English, and other languages can illustrate. But it doesn't have to be built from syllable patterns, and it was not so constituted in the English from which Middle English meter evolved. The regular and recurring unit within the metrical line then was English (and Germanic) in nature, and it cannot be represented accurately in units alien to that language. That unit, rather, was based initially on regular recurrence of prosodic stress accent. The number of syllables between these accents may be several—

> Gábriel hire grétte and séyde hire, "Avé!
> Márie ful of gráce, oure Lórd be wyth thée" (**10**.9–10)

or they may be few—

> Whan mén beth múriest át her méle
> Wyth méte and drýnke to máken hem gláde (**43**.1–2)

or the intervals may be filled regularly with single unstressed syllables—

> The fírste dáy whan Críst was bórn,
> Ther spróng a róse out óf a thórn (**83**.1–2).

While there is much variation in the patterning of stressed and unstressed syllables in these three examples, making it nearly meaningless to compare their metrical "feet," they all show regularity in employing a prosodic pattern quite common throughout Middle English—the grouping of four stress accents to form a verse line.

The metrical unit may be better grasped, perhaps, when it is thought of as a "measure," as in the terminology of music. Measures are the smallest timed units, and it matters not at all whether they are duple, triple, quintuple, or other. If one tries the notion of measure, there may be further help in comprehending the meter of Middle English. If a line is analyzed as having a certain number of measures, nothing is implied about the patterns of syllables within those units. All that is implied is that the same number of stress accents fall at regularized intervals. This is clearest in songs or songlike texts such as **57**—

> Yonge mén, I wárne you éverichóon,
> Élde wýves táketh ye nón (**57**.1–2)

or in stylized, sententious verses, such as **26**—

> Érthe took of érthe, érthe wyth wógh;
> Érthe other érthe to the érthe dróugh (**26**.1–2)

or better still, the only way to read the text of **2** is not by syllable count, but by native English phrase stress regularized:

> Mýrie it ís whil sómer ylást
> Wyth fóweles sóng;
> Bút now néigheth wýndes blást
> And wéder stróng (**2**.1–4)

At the same time it should be recognized that foot measure was introduced early, in imitation of Latin texts (and often in translating them), using English syllable length and stress accent. It developed fairly rapidly, eventually dominating the original meter of English (though never quite displacing it). That is the reason that many more of the later texts in this collection exemplify foot meter than do the earlier ones. And this development coincided generally with loss of syllabic unstressed final -*e*.

Wyth fávour ín her fáce fer pássyng mý resóun (**86**.1)

O Móder mýlde, Mayde úndefíled (**90**.1)

That hérte myn hérte hath ín swich gráce (**100**.1)

But that is how the meter of Middle English ended, not how it began.

Finally, a suggestion. None of the metrical forms should be characterized as, say, "jaunty" or "solemn" or "playful," with such a term used then as a basis for interpretation of the relation of content to form of a poem. The meter of

> Whan the turf is thy tour
> And thy put is thy bour (**9**.1–2)

can be called "jaunty" by one person, "sententious" by another, "lugubrious" or "plodding" by still another, and there is no objective way to demonstrate which one should be right; interpretation of the poem will differ, depending on which one of these characterizations of the meter is taken as the right one.

Perhaps the best way to read these Middle English lyrics is much the way any other well-organized poetry is to be read—recognizing the form to be an interplay of meter and syntax. The four-stress line puts severe constraints on the handling of syntax, with much less opportunity for variation than in the five-stress lines of Chaucer and his successors. As noted above, line endings in this four-stress poetry typically coincide with the completion of a syntactic phrase. This is a revealing dynamic when gauging a poem's metrical success. If the metrical structure and syntatic pattern are mechanically matched (as **49**) the resulting poem will be little more than moral instruction. If it is varied a bit within a plain form (as **100**, or **66** or **67**) it may be clever, often engaging. If it has simple metrical form and explicit progression (as **21**) it can be effective. If it combines a starkly simple metrical form, a patterned simple syntax, and a profound meditation (as **4**) it can be very moving, or it can be learned, allusive, and moving (as **54**). It can be complex in meter, and leave a deep impression (as **77**). It can be elusive and unforgettable at the same time (as **37**). Or it can be simple in form and yet survive for centuries and finally become a topic of endless explication (as **99**).

l

Appendix

Here are transcriptions of two thirteenth-century copies of part of a preaching text (they are drawn from Max Förster, "Kleinere Mittelenglische Texte," *Anglia* 42 (1918), 150-51). Italic type represents expansion of abbreviation symbols.

Also, *crist*ene man and *crist*ene wo*m*man, bote þou ofte þenke o
Also, *crist*ine man 7 *crist*ine wu*mm*a*n*, bute þou ofte þenke of

þe longe stronge pínes, þat I*esu* Crist godis sone drei for þi foule
þe longe stronge pínes, þat I*esu* Crist godes sune drei for þine foule

sínnís, 7 bot þou lete hem for þe loue of hím, þat gaf
si*nn*es, and but tu lete þine fule sínnes for þe luue of hím, þat gaf

his lif 7 his soule for to deliu*er*e þe of þe grisli deth of helle, þat
his lif 7 his soule for to lesín þe ut of þe grislike det of helle, þat

alle weri*n* ide*m*pd to, weílaweí, weílaweí, harde mai þe grisín agein
alle weri*n* dempt to, weilaweí, weilaweí, harde mai þe grisen ageín

þat wrethful dai of dom; þa*n*ne þou salt sen 7 vnd*ir*stondín
þat wrethful dai of dom; þa*n*ne þu schalt sen and vnd*ir*stondi*n*

alle þe pínes 7 te michele maleise, þat I*esu* Crist dreí for þi loue
alle þe pínes 7 te michele meseise, þat I*esu* Crist drei for þí luue

in erþe . O þe ton half þe, o þe toþ*er* half þe, þou schalt sen al
in erþe . O þe ton half þe and o þe toþer half þe, þu schalt se*n* al

rediliche 7 al opínliche biforn al þe werld alle þe sínnís, þat tu
redilike 7 al opinlike biforn al þe werld alle þo ilke sínnes, þat tu

hast don ageínes his forbode wid þout ouþir mid worde, oþir mid
hast don age*n*nis his forbode wid þout oþer wid worde, oþer wid

werk . But it be here þoru verraí penance ibeth, þa*n*ne mattu
werke . But it be hire þoru uerrai pena*n*ce ibet, þa*n*ne maítu

singín 'weilawei, wolawo, þat euere were þou bori*n* oþir biyetín' .
síngín weilawei, wolewo, þat eu*er*e were þou born or biyetín .

Ak, goditot, þa*n*ne is to late, þa*n*ne is te carte atte iyate, and fend
Ak, goditot, ta*n*ne is to late; for þe deuel is

redi þe to takín . Man ware þe .
redi þe to takin . Man, ware þe !

Because these two prose texts are as near to being the same as one is likely to encounter in Middle English, they offer a specially useful exercise in understanding just how various the language and its writing conventions were. Try to catalog all the variants, both between the two versions and within the separate versions. Search, for example, for all the variants of

but ('except, unless')
thou
other ('or')
shalt
-ly/-like
ayen(s)
wyth/mid
or the spelling for /θ/ or /ð/
or occurrence of the "prepositional case" inflection *-e*.

Glosses for these texts that are not contained in the Glossary for this book are listed below in their regularized form.

ac / ak but
bete(n) to remedy, make amends for
biyeten begotten
drei past tense of **drie(n)** to suffer, undergo
forbode prohibition, commandment
goditot = God it wot
grise(n) to quake, shudder
grisly horrible, hideous
lese(n) to set free, deliver
þout thought
verai true
yate gate
weylawey an exclamation of despair

Abbreviations of Titles

EEC	Richard Leighton Greene, *The Early English Carols*, 2d ed., revised and enlarged (Oxford, 1977).
EEL	E. K. Chambers and F. Sidgwick, *Early English Lyrics* (London, 1907).
EL XIII	Carleton Brown, *English Lyrics of the XIIIth Century* (Oxford, 1932).
EMET	Bruce Dickins and R. M. Wilson, *Early Middle English Texts* (London, 1951).
HL	G. L. Brook, *The Harley Lyrics*, 2d ed., revised (Manchester, 1956).
HP XIV-XV	Rossell Hope Robbins, *Historical Poems of the XIVth and XVth Centuries* (New York, 1959).
Index	Carleton Brown and Rossell Hope Robbins, *The Index of Middle English Verse* (New York, 1943); Rossell Hope Robbins and John Levi Cutler, *Supplement to the Index of Middle English Verse* (Lexington, 1965).
LLME	R. M. Wilson, *The Lost Literature of Medieval England*, 2d ed., revised and reset (London, 1970).
MED	*Middle English Dictionary.*
OED	*The Oxford English Dictionary.*
OEM	Richard Morris, *An Old English Miscellany*, Early English Text Society, o. s. 49.
RL XIV	Carleton Brown, *Religious Lyrics of the XIVth Century*, 2d ed., revised by G. V. Smithers (Oxford, 1957).
RL XV	Carleton Brown, *Religious Lyrics of the XVth Century* (Oxford, 1939).
SL XIV-XV	Rossell Hope Robbins, *Secular Lyrics of the XIVth and XVth Centuries* (Oxford, 1952).

TEXTS OF THE LYRICS

A note on the glosses. In addition to translation glosses in roman type, equivalence glosses in Middle English are given occasionally, appearing in italic type following an = sign. Glossed words having special syntactic use can be identified by the *i.e.* that follows the boldface glossed word.

1

Myrie songen the monkes binne Ely
Whan Cnut Kyng rewe ther-by:
Roweth, knightes, neer the lond
4   And here we thise monkes song.

Index 2164. Trinity Coll. Camb. MS. 1105. (J. E. Wells, *A Manual of the Writings in Middle English*, 1050-1400, p. 490.)
One other source. *c.* 1150.

1. **binne** within
2. **rewe** rowed

2

Myrie it is whil somer ylast
Wyth foweles song;
But now neigheth wyndes blast
4   And weder strong.
Ei! Ei! What, this nyght is long,
And I wyth wel muchel wrong
Sorwe and murne and faste.

Index 2163. Rawlinson MS. G. 22 [=Bodl. 14755]. (*EL XIII* No. 7.)
With music. Unique text. *c.* 1225.

1. **ylast** lasts, continues
6. **wyth** because of, as a result of

Somer is i-comen in,
Loude syng cuckow!
Groweth seed and bloweth meed
4 And spryngeth the wode now.
Syng cuckow!
Ewe bleteth after lamb,
Loweth after calve cow;
8 Bullock sterteth, bukke farteth,—
Myrie syng cuckow!
Cuckow! Cuckow!
Wel syngest thou cuckow:
12 Ne swik thou nevere now.
Syng cuckow, now, syng cuckow!
Syng cuckow, syng cuckow, now!

Index 3223. MS. Harley 978. (*EL XIII* No. 6.)
With music. Unique text, 1230–40. *c.* 1225.

1. **somer** spring; **i-comen** is a past participle
3. **bloweth** blows, bursts into flower, blooms
8. **sterteth** starts, leaps; **bukke** buck, stag
12. **swik** cease, stop

4

Now goth sonne under wode,—
Me reweth, Marie, thy faire rode.
Now goth sonne under tree,—
4   Me reweth, Marie, thy sone and thee.

Index 2320.   Bodleian MS. Arch. Selden, supra 74 [= Bodl. 3462]. (*EL XIII* No. 1.)
Contained in over forty MSS. in French, Latin, and English. *c.* 1240.

1. **rode** face, visage

Man may longe lyves wene,
But ofte him lieth the wrench;
Faire weder wendeth ofte into reyn
4 And ferly maketh his blench.
Ther-fore, man, thou thee bithenk,—
Al shal falewe the grene.
Weylawey! nis kyng ne quene
8 That ne shal drynke of Dethes drench.
Man, er thou falle offe thy bench,
Thy synne a-quench.

Ne may strong ne stark ne kene
12 A-glye Dethes wither-clench;
Yong ne old, bright ne shene,
Alle he riveth in his strengthe.
Fous and ferly is the wrench,
16 Ne may him no man ther-toyeins—

Index 2070. Maidstone MS. A. 13, Laud Misc. 471 [= Bodl. 1053]. (*EL XIII* No. 10A, 10B).

Redacted from the two texts cited, with variants, as noted, from Cotton MS. Caligula ix and Jesus Coll. Oxf. MS. 29 (*OEM* XX). Four full texts. With music. *c.* 1250.

1. **lyves** life. *Wene* here has its object in the genitive case. The line means: "Man may expect to have a long life."
2. **him lieth the wrench** for him a deception (or sudden turning) lies in wait
4. **ferly maketh his blench** suddenly, wonderfully plays his trick
6. **falewe** wither, fade
8. **drench** drink, draught
12. **A-glye Dethes wither-clench** escape Death's hostile grasp
14. **riveth** tears apart
15. **Fous and ferly** ready and sudden, eager and terrible
16. **ther-toyeins** *i.e.,* (act) in opposition to

Weylawey! wepyng ne bene,
  Mede, list, ne leches drench.
  Man, lat synne and lustes stench;
20 Wel do, wel thenk.

Do by Salomones rede,
  Man, and so thou shalt wel do;
Do as he thee taughte and seyde
24 What thyn cndyng thee bryngeth to,
  Ne shalt thou nevere mys-do.
Sore thou myghte thee adrede,
Weylawey! swich weneth wel lede
28 Long lyf and blisse under-fo;
  But Deeth luteth in his sho
  To him for-do.

Man, why n'iltow thee biknowe?
32 Man, why n'iltow thee bisee?
Of filthe thou are issue—
  Wormes mete thou shalt be.
  Heer navest thou blisse dayes three,
36 But al thy lyf thou dreyest in wo.
Weylawey! Deeth thee shal doun throwe
  Ther thou wenest heighe stye;
  In wo shal thy wcle ende,
40 In wop thy glee.

17. **bene** prayer, supplication
18. **list** craft, cunning
28. **under-fo** receive
29. **luteth in his sho** lurks in his shoe. *But* supplied (for *ac*) from Cotton Caligula and Jesus Coll. Oxf. MSS.
30. **for-do** destroy
28. **navest** = *ne havest, ne hast*
36. **dreyest** endure, suffer
38. **ther** i.e., there where; **stye** climb, ascend
40. **wop** lamentation, weeping

World and wele thee biswiketh;
 Y-wis, they ben thy fo!
If the world wyth wele thee sliketh,
44 That is for to don thee wo.
 Ther-fore lat lust over-go,
Man, and eft it thee liketh.
Weylawey! how sore him wiketh
48 Ther in oon stounde or two
 He werketh him pyne evermo.
 Ne do thou so!

41. **biswiketh** deceives
43. **sliketh** flatters
47. **wiketh** yields, fails

6

If man him bithoghte
Inwardly and ofte
How hard is the fore
4 From bed to floor,
How reweful is the flitte
From floor to pitte,
From pitte to pyne
8 That never shal fyne,—
I wene non synne
Sholde his herte wynne.

Index 1422. Arundel MS. 292. (*EL XIII* No. 13.)

Many other texts, variants, versions; as mural inscription and as tombstone inscription: thirteenth to sixteenth centuries. *c.* 1250.

2. **inwardly** earnestly; MS. *inderlike*
3. **fore** going, journey
5. **flitte** departing, removal
6. **pitte** pit, grave
8. **fyne** end, finish

Have oon god in worshipe,
Ne nem thou his name in idelshipe,
Wite wel thyn holy-day,
4 Fader and moder worship ay;
Loke that thou ne slee no man,
Ne synne by non womman;
Fals oth that thou ne swere,
8 Fals witnesse that thou ne bere;
Non mannes wyf after longe,
Ne of his thyng to han wyth wronge.

Thise ben Goddes bodes ten
12 That shullen kepen alle men:
They that nollen hem ykepe,
They shullen into helle depe;
They that kepen hem aright,
16 They shullen into hevene bright.

Index 1129. Trinity Coll. Camb. MS. 323. (*EL XIII* No. 23.)
Eight versions, largely independent of each other. *c.* 1250.

 2. **nem** call, name; **idelshipe** idleness, vain
10. **wyth wronge** wrongfully
11. **bodes** commands, commandments
13. **nollen** = *ne wollen*

Sey me, wight in the broom,
Teche me how I shal don
That myn housebonde
4 Me loven wolde.

"Hold thy tonge stille
And have al thy wylle."

Index 3078. Trinity Coll. Camb. MS. 323. (*EL XIII* No. 21.)
One other text. *c.* 1250.

1. **broom** broom, brushwood

9

Whan the turf is thy tour
And thy put is thy bour,
Thy fel and thy white throte
4   Shullen wormes to note.
What helpeth thee than
Al the worlde wenne?

Index 4044. Trinity Coll. Camb. MS. 323. (*EL XIII* No. 30.)
Unique text; directly translated from Latin verses. *c.* 1250.

2. **put** = *pit*, i.e., grave
3. **fel** skin
4. **Shullen wormes to note** worms shall have for their use (or purpose)
6. **worlde wenne** joys, pleasures of the world; (?) to win the world

10

Now thise foweles syngen and maken her blisse,
And that gras up thryngeth and leveth the rys;
Of oon I wyl synge that is makeles,
4   The kyng of alle kynges to moder He hire ches.

She is wythouten synne and wythouten hore,
I-comen of kynges kyn of Jesses more;
The lord of mankynde of hire was i-born
8   To brynge us out of synne, elles we weren forlorn.

Gabriel hire grette and seyde hire, "Ave!
Marie ful of grace, oure Lord be wyth thee;
The fruyt of thy womb i-blessed moot it be.
12   Thou shalt gon wyth childe, for sothe I seye it thee."

Whan that gretyng that aungel hadde i-broght,
She gan to bithenke and meinde hir thoght;
She seyde to the aungel, "How may tiden this?
16   Of mannes y-mone not I noght, y-wis."

Index 2366. Trinity Coll. Camb. MS. 323. (*EL XIII* No. 31.)
Unique text. *c.* 1250.

2. **leveth the rys** the small branch (of a bush) puts forth leaves
4. **ches** chose; **kyng** for MS. *kind*
5. **hore** stain, defilement
6. **more** stock, root
12. **for sothe** forsooth, for truth
13. *Whan* replaces MS. *and*
14. **meinde** mingled, disturbed
15. **tiden** betide, come to pass; **How** for MS. *þu*
16. **y-mone** company, intercourse; **not** = *ne wot* know not

Mayden she was wyth childe and mayden heer-biforn,
And mayden er sith-that hir child was i-born;
Mayden and moder nas nevere non womman but she:
20 Wel myghte she berere of Goddes sone be.

I-blessed be that swete child and the moder eke,
And the swete brest that hir sone seek;
I-heried be the tyme that swich child was i-born,
24 That lesed al of pyne that erre was forlorn.

19. *nas = ne was*
20. **she** (= *he* in the original dialect) for MS. *þe*
22. **seek** sucked
24. **lesed** loosed released, delivered; **erre** before, formerly

11

Of oon that is so faire and bright
Velud maris stella,
Brighter thanne the dayes light,
4   *Parens et puella:*
I crie to thee, thou see to me,
Lady, preye thy Sone for me,
Tam pia,
8 That I moot come to thee,
Maria.

Of care counseil thou art best;
Felix fecundata.
12 Of alle wery thou art reste,
Mater honorata.
Biseech thou Him wyth mylde mood,
That for us alle shedde his blood
16 *In cruce.*
That we moten come to Him
In luce.

Index 2645. Egerton MS. 613, and Trinity Coll. Camb. MS. 323. (*EL XIII* No. 17A, 17B.)
The text here follows the Egerton MS. except as noted. *c.* 1250.

2. **Velud maris stella** as the star of the sea
4. **Parens et puella** i.e., *moder and mayden*
7. **Tam pia** you who are so gracious
9. **Maria** Mary
10. **counseil** consolation
11. **Felix fecundata** i.e., blessed is the fruit of thy womb
13. **Mater honorata** mother (who is) honored
14. *thou* not in Egerton MS.
16. **In cruce** on the cross
18. **In luce** in the light

Al this world was forlorn
20   *Eua peccatrice,*
Til oure Lord was i-born
    De te genetrice.
Wyth *Aue* it went awey
24   Thester nyght and cam the day
    Salutis;
The welle spryngeth out of thee
    Uirtutis.

28   Lady, flour of alle thyng,
    Rosa sine spina,
Thou bare Jhesu, hevenes kyng
    Gratia divina.
32   Of alle thou berest the pris,
Lady, quene of paradys
    Electa,
Moder mylde and mayden eke
36   *Effecta.*

20. **Eua peccatrice** through Eve (being) a sinner; because Eve sinned
22. **De te genetrice** i.e., from you His mother
24. **Thester** dark; *cam,* based on T.C.C. MS., replaces Egerton MS. *comet*
25. **Salutis** of safety, of salvation
27. **Uirtutis** of virtue
29. **Rosa sine spina** rose without thorn
31. **Gratia divina** by divine grace
34. **Electa** elected, the elected one
35. *Moder mylde and mayden eke* follows T.C.C. MS., replacing Egerton MS. *Mayde milde Moder es.*
36. **Effecta** created

Wel He wot He is thy sone
Uentre quem portasti;
He wyl not werne thee thy boon
40   *Paruum quem lactasti.*
So hende and so good He is,
He hath broght us alle to blisse
Superni,
44   That hath i-dut the foule put
Inferni.

38. **Uentre quem portasti** whom you carried in your belly
39. **werne** refuse
40. **Paruum quem lactasti** whom you suckled when small
42. *alle* not in Egerton MS.
43. **Superni** on high
44. **i-dut** closed, shut; **put** = *pit* grave
45. **Inferni** below

On hire is al my lyf ylong
Of whom I wylle synge,
And herien hire ther-among
4   That gan us boot brynge
Of helle-pyne that is strong,
And broghte us blisse that is long,
Al thurgh hir childyng.
8   I bidde hire in my song
She yeve us good endyng,
Thogh we don wrong.

Al this world, it shal a-go
12   Wyth sorwe and wyth sore;
And al this blisse we shullen forgo,
Ne of-thinken it us so sore:
This world nis but oure fo.

Index 2687. Trinity Coll. Camb. MS. 323, with variants based on (C)
Cotton MS. Caligula A. ix; (R) Royal MS. 2.F.viii; (J) Jesus Coll.
Oxf. MS. 29. (*EL XIII* No. 32A, 32B, 32C, and *OEM* No. XXI.)
Four texts, with different order of stanzas. *c.* 1250.

1. **ylong** dependent
3. **ther-among** i.e., in the course of my singing; *hire* from C, R, J, for MS.
   him
4. **boot** salvation, redress
6. *so* omitted before *long*, as in C, R, J.
7. **childyng** child-bearing
8. *I* and *my* from C, R, J, for MS. *We* and *ure*
11. **a-go** pass away (utterly)
12. **sore** (noun) pain, grief, suffering
13. *we shullen* from C, R, J, for MS. *ic mot*
14. **Ne of-thinken . . . us** we should not regret, grieve about, repent;
    sore (adverb); *it, us* from C, R, J, for MS. *me*

16   Ther-fore I wyl hennes go
And lernen Goddes lore;
This worldes blisse nis worth a slo—
I bidde, God, thyn ore,
20   Now and evermore.

To long I have sot i-be;
Ful sore I me adrede;
I-loved I have gamen and glee
24   And evere faire wede.
Al that nis noght, ful wel I see,
Ther-fore I wyl hem flee
And lete myn sot-hede.
28   I bidde hire me on to see
That can wisse and rede,
That is so free.

Thou art hele and lyf and light
32   And helpest al mankynne;
Thou us hast ful wel i-dight,
Thou yafe us wele and wynne.
Thou broghtest day and Eve nyght;
36   She broghte wo, thou broghest right;

18. **slo** sloe, blackthorn berry
21. **sot** foolish
22. **me adrede** (reflexive verb) I am afraid
24. **wede** clothing, garments
26. *I wyl hem*, based on R, for MS. *we sulin ur sunnis*
27. **sot-hede** foolishness, folly; *lete myn*, based on R, for MS. *ure*
28. **see** watch over; *I* and *me* based on C and R, for MS. *we* and *us*; *on* not in MS.
29. **wisse and rede** direct, guide, and counsel
31. *Thou*, here and subsequently, from C, R, J, for MS. *Heo/Ho*

19

Thou almesse and she synne.
Bisee to me, lady brighte,
Whan I shal wende henne—
40 Ful wel thou myghte.

Agulte I have, weylawey!
Synful I am and wrecche!
Thou do me mercy, swete lady,
44 Er deeth me hennes fecche.
Yef me thy love, I am redy,
Lat me lyve and amendy
That fendes me ne lette;
48 For my synnes I am sory,
Of my lyf I ne recche.
Lady, mercy!

37. **almesse** charity, charitable gifts
38. **Bisee** give heed to, attend to; *Bisee to me*, based on C, R, J, for MS.
þu do us merci
39. **wende henne** = *wende hennes*, i.e., die; *I shal*, from C, R, J, for MS.
we sulin henne
41. **Agulte** offended, been guity, been sinful
43. *swete lady*, from R, for MS. *lauedi brit*
46. **amendy** = *amende*
47. **lette** hinder, cut off
48. **For** for MS. *of*, as in other versions
49. **recche** care for, have regard for

13

Whoso saw on rode
Jhesus his lemman,—
Sory stood him by wepynge
4 Seint Marie and Seint John,—
His hed him al aboute
Wyth thornes i-prikcd,
His faire hondes and his faire feet
8 Wyth nayles i-stiked,
His rigge wyth yerdes swongen,
His side wyth spere i-wounded -
Al for synne of man:
12 Sore he may wepe
And bittre teres lete,
Man that of love can.

Index 4141. Trinity Coll. Camb. MS. 323. (*EL XIII* No. 34.)
Unique text, *c.* 1250, but see other versions following.

9. **rigge** back; **yerdes** rods

14

14A

Whan I see on rode i-don
Jhesus my lemman,
And by him stonden
4 Marie and Iohan,
His herte depe i-stongen,
His body wyth scourge i-swongen
For the synne of man:
8 Ethe I may wepe
And salte teres lete
If I of love can.

14B

Whan I see on rode
Jhesu my lemman,
And biside him stonden
4 Marie and Iohan,
And his rigge i-swongen,
And his side i-stongen
For the love of man:
8 Wel owe I to wepe
And synnes forlete,
If I of love can,
If I of love can,
12 If I of love can.

Index 3965. (A) St. John's Coll. Camb. MS. 15; *Index* 3964. (B) Royal
MS. 12. E. i. (*EL XIII* No. 35A, 35B.)
Unique versions. Early fourteenth century.

A. 6. *wyth* for MS. *þis*
   8. **ethe** easily, readily

B. 5. **rigge** back

15

Whan I on the rode see
Faste nayled to the tree
Jhesu my lemman,
4 I-bounde blak and blody,
And his moder stonde him by
Wepying and Iohan;

His bak wyth scourge i-swongen,
8 His side depe i-stongen
For synne and love of man:
Wel oghte I synne lete
And neb wyth teres wete,
12 If I of love can.

Index 3961. MS. Bodleian 57 [= Bodl. 2004]. (*EL XIII* No. 36.)
Unique version. *c.* 1300.

4. **blak** pale
11. **neb** face

16

Whan I thenke on the rode
Wher-upon thou stood,
   Swete Jhesu my lemman;
4 How by thee was stondyng
Thy moder wepyng
   And thy disciple Seint Iohan;
How thy rigge was i-swongen,
8 And thy side thurgh-stongen
   For the gilt of man;
How thy feet y-bledden,
And thyne hondes y-spredden
12   That they myghten telle thy bon;
How the stones to-breken,
The dede arisen and speken,
   The sonne wex al wan:
16 No sely thogh I wepe
And my synnes bete
   If I of love can.

Index 3968. MS. Ashmole 360 [= Bodl. 6641]. (*EL XIII* No. 37.)
Unique version. Thirteenth century.

7. **rigge** back
12. **telle** count; **ban** is plural
13. **to-breken** broke to pieces
16. **sely** wonder, marvel
17. **bete** amend, make amends for

17

Foweles in the frith,
The fisshes in the flood,
And I mon waxe wood:
4 Muche sorwe I walke wyth
For best of bon and blood.

Index 864. MS. Douce 139 [= Bodl. 21713]. (*EL XIII* No. 8.)
With music. Unique text. *c.* 1270.

1. **frith** woodland, forest
3. **mon** must
5. **best** i.e., the best (person)

18

Wher beth they biforn us weren,
Houndes ladden and haukes beren
And hadden feeld and wode?
4 The riche ladies in her bour
That wereden gold in her tresour,
Wyth her brighte rode?

They eten and dronken and maden hem glad—
8 Her lyf was al wyth gamen i-lad;
Men kneleden hem biforn;
They beren hem wel swithe heighe,
And in a twynkelyng of an eye
12 Her soules weren forlorn.

Wher is that laughyng and that song,
That trailyng and that proude yong,
Tho haukes and tho houndes?
16 Al that joye is went awey—
That wele is comen to weylawey,
To many harde stoundes.

Index 3310. MS. Digby 86 [= Bodl. 1687]. (*EL XIII* No. 48.)
Also in Vernon MS., MS. Harley 2253, and MS. Laud 108 [= Bodl.
1486], all three printed in *The Minor Poems of the Vernon MS*, ed.
F. J. Furnivall, EETS o.s. 117, pp. 518–22. *c.* 1270.

5. **tresour** headdress
6. **rode** face, countenance
7. *They* supplied from other MSS.
14. **trailyng** long, trailing garments; **yong** walk, gait
16. **went** turned, gone

Her paradys they nomen heer,
20 And now they liggen in helle y-fere;
The fyr it brenneth evere.
Long is ay and long is o,
Long is wei and long is wo—
24 Thennes ne comen they nevere.

Drey heer, man, than if thou wylt
A litel pyne that me thee bit;
Wythdraw thyne eses ofte.
28 Thogh thy pyne be unrede,
And thou thenke on thy mede
It shal thee thynken softe.

If that feend, that foule thyng,
32 Thurgh wikked roun, thurgh fals eggyng,
Nethere thee hath i-cast,
Up and be good champioun!
Stond, ne fal namore adoun
36 For a litel blast!

Thou tak the rode to thy staf,
And thenk on him that there-on yaf
His lyf that was so leef.

19. **nomen** took, seized
20. **liggen** lie; **y-fere** together, in company
25. **Drey** endure, suffer
26. **me thee bit** one (anyone) bids you; men bid you
27. **eses** comforts
28. **unrede** severe
29. **and** if
32. **roun** advice
33. **nethere** down, downward

40 He it yaf for thee, thou yeld it him:
    Ayeins his fo that staf thou nim
    And wrek him of that theef.

    Of right bileve, thou nim that sheeld
44 The whiles that thou best in that feeld,
    Thyn hond to strengthen fond!
    And keep thy fo wyth staves ord,
    And do that traytour seyn that word:
48 Biget that myrie lond!

    Ther-inne is day withouten nyght,
    Wythouten ende strengthe and myght,
    And wreche of every fo;
52 Wyth God him-selve eche lyf,
    And pees and reste wythouten strif—
    Wele wythouten wo.

    Mayden modor, hevenes quene,
56 Thou myghte and canst and owest to ben
    Oure sheeld ayeins the feend.
    Help us synne for-to fleen,
    That we mote thy sone seen
60 In joye wythouten ende. Amen.

40. **thou yeld it him** repay him for it
41. **nim** seize, take
42. **wrek** avenge
45. **fond** try, attempt
46. **ord** point (?); the sense of this line is "meet thy foe with opposition"
47. **word** i.e., word of surrender
48. **Biget** attain, get
51. **wreche** vengeance
52. **eche** eternal

19

"Stond wel, Moder, under rode,
Bihold thy child wyth gladde mood;
4 Blithe, Moder, myghtestow be."
"Sone, how may I blithe stond?
I see thy feet, I see thyne honde
Nayled to the harde tree."

"Moder, do wey thy wepyng,
8 I thole this deeth for mannes thyng;
For my gilt ne thole I non."
"Sone, I fele the dethes stounde;
That swerd is at myn hertes grounde,
12 That me bihete Simeon."

"Moder, rewe upon thy bern;
Thou wassh awey the blody teren:
It doth me worse thanne my deeth."

Index 3211. MS. Digby 86 [= Bodl. 1687]. (*EL XIII* No. 49A.)
With variants from (R) Royal MS. 12.E.i, with music (*EL XIII* No.
49B); (H) MS. Harley 2253 (*HL* No. 20); and (J) St. John's Coll.
Camb. MS. 111, with music (*EL XIII* pp. 203–4). Five full versions.
c. 1270.

3. MS. *Moder bliþe*; R, H, J *Bliþe moder*
5. **honde** = *hondes.* Line based on R and H, for MS. *Ich se þine fet and þine honde.*
8. Line based on R, for MS. *Ich þolie deþ for monnes kuinde.*
13. **bern** son. Line based on R, for MS. *Moder, do wei þine teres.*
14. **teren** = *teres.* Line based on R and H, for MS. *þou wip awey þe blodi teres.*

16   "Sone, how myghte I teres werne?
     I see thy blody woundes erne
     From thyn herte to my feet."

     "Moder, now I may thee seye,
20   Bettre is that ich oone deye
     Thanne al mankynde to helle go."
     "Sone, I see thy body i-swongen—
     Thy brest, thyne honde, thy feet thurgh-stongen:
24   No sely is thogh me be wo."

     "Moder, if I thee durste telle,
     If I ne deye thou gost to helle;
     I thole this deeth for mannes sake."
28   "Sone, thou best so meke and mynde,
     Ne wyte me noght—it is my kynde
     That I for thee this sorwe make."

     "Moder, mercy! lat me deye
32   And Adam out of helle beye,
     And al mankynde that is forlorn."
     "Sone, what shal me to rede?
     Thy pyne pyneth me to dede:
36   Lat me deye thee biforn."

16. **werne** restrain
17. **erne** run, flow
18. *my feet,* based on R and H, for MS. *þy fot*
23-24. Based on R, for MS. *þine honde, þine fet, þi bodi I-stounge; / Hit nis
no wonder þey me be wo.* **sely** wonder, marvel
27. *this* supplied from R
28-30. Lines based on R and H, for MS. *Sone, þou bi-hest so milde; / I-comen
hit is of monnes kuinde / þat ich sike and serewe make.*
28. **mynde** mindful, thoughtful
29. **wyte** blame
33. *al* supplied from R
34-35. Lines based on R and H, for MS. *Sone, wat sal mc þe stounde? / þine
pinen me bringeþ to þe grounde.* **dede** = *death*

"Moder, now thou myghte wel lernen
What pyne tholen that children beren,
What sorwe han that child forgon."

40 "Sone, I wot I may thee telle
But it be the pyne of helle;
Of more pyn ne wot I non."

"Moder, rewe of modres care
44 Now thou wost of modres fare,
Thogh thou be clene mayden-man."
"Sone, thou helpest at the nede
Alle tho that to thee grede,
48 Mayden, wyf, and fole womman."

"Moder, I may no lenger dwelle—
The tyme is comen I shal to helle:
The thridde day I rise upon."
52 "Sone, I wyl wyth thee founden,
I deye y-wis of thyne wounden;
So reweful deeth was nevere non."

37-39. Lines based on R and H, for MS. *Swete moder, nou þou fondest* / *Of my pine, þer þou stondest; Wiþ-houte mi pine nere no mon.*
39. **forgon** relinquish, forego, lose
43-48. Lines based on R, for MS. *Moder, of moder þus I fare.* / *Nou þou wost wimmanes kare,* / *þou art clene mayden on.* / *Sone, þou helpest alle nede,* / *Alle þo þat to þe wille grede,* / *May and wif and fowel wimmon.*
44. **fare** lot, fate
45. **mayden-man** a maiden, virgin
47. **grede** call out, pray, cry
48. **fole** foolish
50. *shal* from H, for MS. go
51-54. Lines based on R, for MS. *I þolie þis for þine sake.* / *Sone, I-wis I wille founde,* / *I deye almest, I falle to grounde,* / *So serwful deþ nes never non.*
52. **founden** depart, leave, go away
53. **wounden** = *woundes*

Whan he ros than fil hir sorwe;
56   The blisse sprong the thridde morwe.
Blithe moder were thou tho!
Lady, for that ilke blisse,
Biseech thy Sone oure synnes lisse;
60   Thou be oure sheeld ayeins oure fo.

Blessed be thou, quene of hevene!
Bryng us out of helle levene
Thurgh thy dere sones myght.
64   Moder, for that heighe blood
That He shedde upon the rode,
Leed us into hevenes light.

55-66. Based on R and H; absent in MS. Digby 86
59. **synnes lisse** remission of sins
62. **helle levene** the lightning, flame, of hell

20

Ne hath my soule but fyr and yse
And the lichame erthe and tree:
Bidde we alle the heighe kyng
4 That welde shal the laste doom
That he us lete that ilke thyng,
That we mowen his wylle don;
He us skere of the tithyng
8 That synfulle shullen an-underfon,
Whan deeth hem ledeth to the myrthe
That nevere ne beth undon.   Amen.

Index 2284.5. Jesus Coll. Oxf. MS. 29. (*OEM* No. XII.) *c.* 1275.

2. **lichame** body
4. **welde** wield, rule over
7. **skere of the tithyng** free (or excuse) from the wages (reward)
8. **an-underfon** receive
9. **myrthe** reward, pay

21

Whan I thenke thynges three
Ne may I nevere blithe be:
That oon is that I shal awey;
4   That other is I ne wot which day;
The thridde is my moste care—
I ne wot whider I shal fare.

Index 3969. New Coll. Oxf. MS. 88 and Arundel MS. 292. (*EL XIII* No. 12A, 12B.)
Three other texts of this version; also, other versions. *c.* 1300.

22

Lord, thou clepedest me,
And I noght ne answerde thee
But wordes slowe and slepy:
4   "Thole yet! Thole a litel!"
But "yet" and "yet" was endeles,
And "thole a litel" a long weye is.

Index 1978. New Coll. Oxf. MS. 88. (*RL XIV* No. 5.)
Unique text. *c.* 1300.

23

    Wel, who shal thise hornes blowe
      Holy Rode thy day?
    Now is he deed and lieth lowe
4   Was wont to blowe hem ay.

Index 3894 (but *Supplement* 3857.5). Lansdowne MS. 207(e). (*EMET* p. 118.)

After 1280.

2. **Holy Rode thy day** Holy Cross Day, the feast of the Exaltation of the Cross (September 14)

24

    Myrie a tyme I telle in May
      Whan brighte blosmes breken on tree;
    This foweles syngen nyght and day:
4   In ilke grene is gamen and glee.

Index 2162. Pembroke Coll. Camb. MS. 258. (*SL XIV-XV* No. 141.)
Unique text. *c.* 1300.

2. **breken** burst into flower
4. **ilke grene** each green, grassy spot

Now spryngeth the spray,
Al for love I am so sik
That slepen I ne may.

As I me rod this endre day
  On my pleyinge,
Saw I where a litel may
4   Bigan to synge:
  "The clot him clynge!
Wei is him in love-longynge
  Shal lyven ay:
8   Now spryngeth the spray,
      Al for love I am so sik
      That slepen I ne may."

Soon I herde that myrie note
12   Thider I drough;
I fond hire in an herber swote
  Under a bough,
  Wyth joye ynough.
16 Soon I axed: "Thou myrie may,
  Why syngestow ay
    'Now spryngeth the spray,
    Al for love I am so sik
20   That slepen I ne may?'"

Index 360. Lincoln's Inn MS. Hale 135. (*EL XIII* No. 62.)
Unique text. *c.* 1300.

  5. **The clot him clynge** may the clay cling to him, i.e., would that he were dead
  6. **Wei is him** woe be to (*or* there is woe for) him who
11. **Soon** as soon as
13. **swote** = *swete* pleasant

Than answerde that mayden swote
Wyth wordes fewe:
"My lemman me haveth bihote
24   Of love trewe;
He chaungeth anew.
If I may, it shal him rewe
By this day."
28   *Now spryngeth the spray,*
Al for love I am so sik
That slepen I ne may.

26

Erthe took of erthe, erthe wyth wogh;
Erthe other erthe to the erthe drough;
Erthe leyde erthe in erthen through:
4   Than hadde erthe of erthe erthe ynough.

Index 3939. MS. Harley 2253. (*EL XIII* No. 73.)
Many variants, versions, and expansions. *c.* 1320.

1. **wogh** wrong, harm
2. **drough** drew, added
3. **through** coffin, grave

Bitwene March and Aperil,
Whan spray bigynneth to sprynge,
The litel fowel hath hir wyl
4   On hir lede to synge.
I lyve in love-longynge
For semlokest of alle thyng;
She may me blisse brynge:
8   I am in hir baundoun.
     An hende hap I have i-hent,
     I wot from hevene it is me sent;—
     From alle wommen my love is lent
12   And light on Alysoun.

On hewe hir heer is faire ynough,
Hir browes broune, hir eyen blake,
Wyth lufsom chere she on me lough,
16   Wyth middel smal and wel i-mak.

Index 515. MS. Harley 2253. (*EL XIII* No. 77.)
Unique text. *c.* 1320.

4. **lede** language
6. **semlokest** seemliest, most fair
8. **baundoun** power, control, i.e., at her disposal
9. **An hende hap I have i-hent** I have received (obtained) a gracious
fortune; I have got a piece of good luck
11. **lent** taken away, gone
14. *browes, eyen* are given their normal plural inflexions here, for plural forms
in MS. *browe* and *eʒe*
15. **Wyth lufsom chere she on me lough** with a lovely face she smiled
on me

But she me wol to hire take
For-to ben hir owene make,
Longe to lyve I wyl forsake
20 And feye falle adoun.
　　An hende hap I have i-hent,
　　I wot from hevene it is me sent;—
　　From alle wommen my love is lent
24 　　And light on Alysoun.

Nyghtes whan I wende and wake—
For-thy my wonges waxen wan;
Lady, al for thy sake
28 Longyng is i-lent me on.
In world nis non so witter man
That al hir bountee telle can:
Hir swire is whiter thanne the swan,
32 And fairest may in toun.
　　An hende hap I have i-hent,
　　I wot from hevene it is me sent;—
　　From alle wommen my love is lent
36 　　And light on Alysoun.

20. **feye** doomed (to die)
25. **wende** turn (and toss)
26. **wonges** cheeks
28. **i-lent** come upon
29. **witter** wise
30. **bountee** excellence, virtue
31. **swire** neck
32. **fairest** (she is the) fairest

I am for wowyng al forwake,
Wery as water in wore;
Lest any reve me my make
40 I have i-yerned yore.
Bettre is tholen while sore
Thanne murnen evermore.
Geynest under gore,
44 Herkne to my roun:
An hende hap I have i-hent,
I wot from hevene it is me sent;—
From alle wommen my love is lent
48 And light on Alysoun.

37. **forwake** overwatched, worn out with lying awake
38. **wore** troubled pool (?); *so* for MS. *as*
43. **Geynest under gore** kindest in gown, i.e., of all women, of any alive
44. **roun** song

28

Lenten is comen wyth love to toun,
Wyth blosmes and wyth briddes roun,
  That al this blisse bryngeth;
4 Dayesyes in thise dales,
Notes swete of nyghtengales—
  Ech fowel song syngeth.
The thrustelcok him threteth oo;
8 Awey is here wynter wo
  Whan woderove spryngeth.
Thise foweles syngen ferly fele
And wlyten on her wynne wele
12   That al the wode ryngeth.

The rose raileth hire rode,
The leves on the lighte wode
  Waxen al wyth wylle;
16 The mone mandeth hire blee,
The lilye is lufsom to see,
  The fenel and the fille.

Index 1861. MS. Harley 2253. (*EL XIII* No. 81.)
Unique text. *c.* 1320.

1. **lenten** spring
3. **roun** cry, song
7. **threteth** contends, chides
9. **woderove** woodruff
10. **ferly fele** wondrously many
11. **wlyten** pipe, warble; **wynne wele** (for MS. *wynter wele*) wealth of joy
13. **raileth hire rode** puts forth her blushing countenance
16. **mandeth hire blee** sends forth her light, radiance

Wowen thise wilde drakes;
20 Miles myrien here makes,
As streem that striketh stille.
Mody meneth, so doth mo;
I wot I am oon of tho,
24 For love that liketh ille.

The mone mandeth hire light
So doth the seemly sonne bright,
Whan briddes syngen breme;
28 Dewes donken thise dounes,
Deres wyth her derne rounes
Domes for-to deme.
Wormes wowen under cloude,
32 Wommen waxen wonder proude,
So wel it wol hem seme.
If me shal wante wylle of oon
This wynne wele I wol forgon
36 And wyght in wode be fleme.

20. **miles myrien** animals (?) gladden
21. **striketh stille** flows softly, quietly
22. **mody meneth** the spirited man laments (complains); **mo** more, i.e., others
27. **breme** clearly, loudly
28. **donken** moisten, dampen
29-30. **Deres wyth her derne rounes / Domes for-to deme** Animals with their cries, unmeaning to us, whereby they converse. (See Kenneth Sisam, ed., *Fourteenth Century Verse and Prose*, p. 256.)
31. **cloude** earth, ground
33. **seme** befit, beseem
36. **wyght** quickly; **fleme** fugitive

29

Blow, Northren Wynd,
Send thou me my swetyng!
Blow, Northren Wynd,
Blow, blow, blow!

    I wot a burde in boure bright
That fully seemly is on sight,
Menskful mayden of myght,
4 Faire and free to fonde;
In al this worthly won
A burde of blood and of bon
Nevere yet I niste non
8 Lufsomer in londe.

    Wyth lokkes leefly and longe,
Wyth frount and face faire to fonde,
Wyth myrthes many moot she monge,
12 That brid so brem in boure;
Wyth lufsom eyen greet and good
Wyth browes blisful under hood—
He that reste him on the rode,
16 That leefly lyf honoure!

Index 1395. MS. Harley 2253. (*EL XIII* No. 83.)
Unique text. *c.* 1320.

  3. **Menskful** noble, honorable, gracious
  4. **fonde** examine; try, test
  5. **worthy won** goodly country
  7. **I niste non** (**niste** = *ne wiste*) never have I known one
  9. **leefly** lovable, delightful, beautiful
10. **frount** forehead
11. **monge** mingle with, i.e., be compared to
12. **brem** bright, splendid

Hire lere lumeth lighte
As a lanterne a-nyghte,
Hir blee bliketh so brighte
20   So faire she is and fyne;
A swetely swire she hath to holde,
Wyth armes, shuldres as man wolde,
And fyngres faire for-to folde—
24   God wolde she were myn!

Myddel she hath menskful smal,
Hir lovely chere as cristal,
Thighes, legges, feet, and al
28   I-wroght was of the best;
A lufsom lady lasteles
That swetyng is and evere was—
A bettre burde nevere nas
32   I-heried wyth the best.

She is dereworthe in day,
Gracious, stout, and gay,
Gentil, joly so the jay,
36   Worthly whan she waketh;
Mayden muriest of mouth,
By est, by west, by north and south
Ther nis fiele ne crouth
40   That swiche myrthes maketh.

17. **lere lumeth** countenance, complexion gleams
19. **blee bliketh** face shines, glistens
21. **swire** neck
25. **menskful smal** gracefully slender
29. **lasteles** faultless
33. **dereworthe** excellent, beloved
36. **worthly** excellent, worthy
39. **fiele, crouth** stringed musical instruments

44

She is coral of goodness,
She is ruby of rightfulnesse,
She is cristal of clennesse,
44 And baner of bealtee;
She is lilye of largesse,
She is pervynke of prowesse,
She is solsecle of sweetnesse,
48 And lady of lealtee.

To Love, that lovely is in londe,
I tolde him as I understonde
How this hende hath hent in honde
52 An herte that myn was;
And hir knightes me han so soght—
Sikyng, Sorwyng, and Thoght—
Tho three me han in bale broght
56 Ayeins the power of Pees.

To Love I putte pleyntes mo,
How Sikyng me hath sewed so,
And eke Thoght me thrat to slo
60 Wyth maistrye if he myghte;
And Sorwe, sore in baleful bend
That he wolde, for this hende,
Me lede to my lyves ende
64 Unlawefully in lighte.

44. **bealtee** beauty
46. **pervynke** periwinkle
47. **solsecle** marigold, heliotrope
48. **lealtee** loyalty, faithfulness
59. **thrat to slo** threatened to slay
61. **bend** bondage, bonds
64. **in lighte** openly

Love me listned ech a word,
And bowed him to me over bord,
And bad me hente that hord
68 Of myn herte hele;
"And biseech that swete and swoot,
Er-than thou falle as fen offe foot,
That she wyth thee wol of boot
72 Dereworthly dele."

For hir love I carke and care,
For hir love I droupe and dare,
For hir love my blisse is bare,
76 And al I waxe wan;
For hir love in sleep I slake,
For hire love al nyght I wake,
For hir love murnyng I make,
80 More thanne any man.

65. MS. *Hire* omitted at beginning of line; *ech a* for MS. *vch.*
67. **hord** treasure
69. **swoot** sweet (one)
70. **fen** mud
71. **boot** deliverance, assistance, remedy
73. **carke and care** sorrow and grieve
74. **droupe and dare** languish and lie timidly

30

Wynter wakeneth al my care;
Now thise leves waxen bare.
Ofte I sike and murne sare
4   Whan it cometh in my thoght
    Of this worldes joye, how it goth al to noght.

Now it is and now it nis,
Also it ner nere, y-wis.
8   That many man seyth, sooth it is—
    Al goth but Goddes wille;
    Alle we shullen deye, thogh us like ille.

Al that greyn me graveth grene,
12   Now it faleweth al bidene.
    Jhesu, help that it be sene,
    And shilde us from helle;
    For I not whider I shal, ne how longe heer dwelle.

Index 4177. MS. Harley 2253. (*RL XIV* No. 9.)
Unique text. *c.* 1320.

3. **sare** = *sore*
7. **ner nere** had never been (*nere* = *ne were*)
11. **greyn me graveth grene** grain (seed) that one buries (plants) green (unripe)
12. **faleweth** withers, fades; **bidene** forthwith, quickly
15. **not** = *ne wot* know not

31

Now shrynketh rose and lilye-flour
That whilom bar that swete savour
   In somer, that swete tide;
4 Ne is no quene so stark ne stour,
Ne no lady so bright in bour,
   That deeth ne shal by glyde.
Whoso wol flesshes lust forgon
8   And hevenes blisse abide,
On Jhesu be his thoght anon,
   That thirled was his side.

From Petresburgh in a morwenynge
12 As I me wende on my pleying,
   On my folye I thoghte;
Menen I gan my murnyng
To hire that bar the hevene kyng,
16   Of mercy hire bisoghte:
Lady, preye thy Sone for us
   That us dere boghte,
And shild us from the lothe hous
20   That to the feend is wroght.

Index 2359. MS. Harley 2253. (*RL XIV* No. 10.)
Unique text. *c.* 1320.

  2. **savour** scent
  9. **anon** continually, constantly
10. **That thirled was his side** whose side was pierced through
13. **folye** wantonness; foolishness; perhaps illicit love
14. **Menen** complain; communicate, declare in lament
19. **lothe hous** hateful, hideous dwelling-place

Myn herte of dedes was fordred
Of synne that I have my flessh fed
And folwed al my tyme,
24 That I not whider I shal be led
Whan I lie on dethes bed—
In joye or into pyne.
On a lady myn hope is,
28   Moder and virgine;
We shullen into hevenes blisse
Thurgh hir medicine.

Bettre is hir medicine
32 Thanne any meed or any wyne;
Hir herbes smellen swete.
From Catenas into Dyvelyn
Nis ther no leche so fyne
36   Oure sorwes to bete.
Man that feleth any sore
And his folye wol lete,
Wythouten gold or any tresour
40   He may be sound and sete.

Of penaunce is his plastre al;
And evere serven hire I shal
Now and al my lyf.
44 Now is free that er was thral,

21. **fordred** terribly frightened
24. **not** = *ne wot* know not
30. **medicine** remedy, cure
34. **From Catenas into Dyvelyn** From Caithness to Dublin
36. **bete** remedy, assuage
37. **sore** pain, grief
40. **sete** content; whole
41. **plastre** (soothing) remedy
44. **thral** enslaved, enthralled

Al thurgh that lady gent and smal—
   Heried be hir joyes five!
Wher-so any sik is,
48   Thider hye blive;
Thurgh hire ben i-broght to blisse
   Bothe mayden and wyf.

For He that dide his body on tree
52   Of oure synnes have pitee
   That weldeth hevenes boures!
Womman wyth thy jolitee—
Thogh thou be white and bright on blee—
56   Thou thenk on Goddes shoures.

. . . .

Falewen shullen thy floures.
Jhesu, have mercy of us,
60   That al this world honoures. Amen.

48. **hye blive** hasten quickly
51. **dide** placed, put
55. **blee** face, complexion. MS. has line sequence 56, 55, 58, 59, 60; the text here follows *RL XIV* No. 10.
56. **shoures** pains, terrors
58. **Falewen** fade, wither
60. **honoures** = *honoreth*

32

Whan the nyghtengale syngeth the wodes waxen grene,
Leef and gras and blosme spryngeth in Aperil, I wene;
And love is to myne herte gon wyth oon spere so kene,
4   Nyght and day my blood it drynketh, myn herte doth me
    tene.

I have loved al this yeer, that I may love namore;
I have siked many sik, lemman, for thyn ore.
Me nis love nevere the neer, and that me reweth sore:
8   Swete lemman, thenk on me,—I have loved thee yore.

Swete lemman, I preye thee of love oon speche;
While I lyve in world so wide other nyl I seche.
Wyth thy love, my swete leef, my blisse thou myghte eche;
12   A swete cosse of thy mouth myghte ben my leche.

Swete lemman, I preye thee of a love-bene;
If thou me lovest, as men seyn—lemman, as I wene—
And if it thy wylle be, thou loke that it be sene.
16   So muche I thenke upon thee that al I waxe grene.

Bitwene Lyncoln and Lindeseye, Northamptoun and
   Lounde
Ne wot I non so faire a may, as I go forbounde.
Swete lemman, I preye thee thou love me a stounde;
20   I wol mone my song on whom that it is on ylong.

Index 4037. MS. Harley 2253. (*EL XIII* No. 86.)
Unique text. *c.* 1320

 4. **doth me tene** causes me suffering
11. **eche** increase
13. **I preye thee of a love-bene** to you I pray for a lovers'-boon
18. **forbounde** (MS. *fore ybounde*) bound, enslaved (by love)
20. **mone** mention; **ylong** due

33

As I me rod this endre day
By grene wode to seche pley,
Wyth herte I thoghte al on a may,
4   Swettest of alle thyng.
Lith and I you telle may
    Al of that swete thyng.

This mayden is swete and free of blood,
8 Bright and faire, of mylde mood;
Al she may don us good
    Thurgh hir bisechyng:
Of hire He took flessh and blood,
12   Jhesus, hevenes kyng.

Wyth al my lyf I love that may;
She is my solas nyght and day,
My joye and eke my beste pley,
16   And eke my love-longynge.
Al the bettre me is that day
    That I of hire synge.

Of alle thyng I love hire mest,
20 My dayes blisse, my nyghtes rest;
She counseileth and helpeth best

Index 359. MS. Harley 2253. (*RL XIV* No. 11.)
Unique text. *c.* 1320

2. **pley** pleasure
5. **Lith** listen
19. **mest** most, to the greatest extent.

Bothe olde and yinge.
Now I may if that you leste
24   The five joyes mynge.

The firste joye of that womman:—
Whan Gabriel from hevene cam
And seyde God sholde bicomen man
28   And of hire be born,
And bryngen up of helle-pyne
Mankynde that was forlorn.

That othere joye of that may
32   Was on Cristemasse day
Whan God was born on thorugh lay
And broghte us lightnesse;
The sterre was seen bifore day—
36   Thise hierdes beren witnesse.

The thridde joye of that lady,
That men clepe the epiphany:—
Whan the kynges comen wery
40   To presente hir sone
Wyth myrre, gold, and encense,
That was man bicome.

22. **yinge** young
23. MS. *nou y may ȝef y wol*; rhyme and meter suggest **If that you leste**
   If it please you or *If that ye leste* If you will listen; the first emendation
   has a formulaic quality and relatively light semantic load to recommend
   it in this context, while the second is recommended by its relation to l. 5.
24. **mynge** mention, call (to mind)
33. **on thorugh lay** in perfect light (?)
34. **lightnesse** light, brightness
36. **hierdes** shepherds

The ferthe joye we telle mowen:
44 On Ester-morwe whan it gan dawen
Hir sone that was slawen
   Aros in flessh and bon;
More joye ne may me haven,
48   Wyf ne mayden non.

The fifte joye of that womman:
Whan hir body to hevene cam
Hir soule to the body nam
52   As it was wont to ben.
Crist leve us all wyth that womman
   That joye al for-to sen.

Preye we alle to oure lady,
56 And to the seintes that wone hire by,
That they of us han mercy,
   And that we ne mysse
In this world to ben holy
60   And wynne hevenes blisse. Amen.

47. **me** one, a person (an indefinite pronoun)
51. **nam** went, drew, took
53. **leve** grant
58. **mysse** miss, fail

54

34

Litel wot it any man
How derne love may stonde,
But it were a free womman
4 That muche of love hadde fonde.
The love of hire ne lasteth nowight longe;
She hath me plight and wyteth me wyth wronge.
Evere and o for my leef I am in grete thoght;
8 I thenke on hire that I ne see not ofte.

I wolde nemne hire to-day
And I durste hire mynne;
She is that fairest may
12 Of ech hende of hir kynne;
But she me love, of me she haveth synne.
Wo is him that loveth the love that he ne may ner
    y-wynne.
Evere and o for my leef I am in grete thoght;
16 I thenke on hire that I ne see not ofte.

Adoun I fil to hire anon
And cried, "Lady, thyn ore!
Lady, have mercy of thy man—
20 Leve thou no fals lore!

Index 1921. MS. Harley 2253. (*EL XIII* No. 91.)
Unique text. *c.* 1320.

2. **derne** secret, not divulged; profound, intense (?)
4. **fonde** had experience with, made trial of
5. **nowight** not a bit, not at all
6. **wyteth me wyth wronge** blames me wrongfully
10. **And** if; **mynne** call to mind
18. *cried* for MS. *cric*
20. **leve** believe

If thou dost it wol me rewe sore.
Love dreccheth me that I ne may lyve namore."
Evere and o for my leef I am in grete thoght;
24   I thenke on hire that I ne see not ofte.

Myrie it is in hir tour
Wyth hatheles and wyth hewes;
So it is in hir bour
28   Wyth gamenes and wyth glewes.
But she me love, sore it wol me rewe.
Wo is him that loveth the love that ner nyl be trewe.
Evere and o for my leef I am in grete thoght;
32   I thenke on hire that I ne see not ofte.

Fairest fode upon-lofte,
My gode leef, I thee grete
As fele sith and ofte
36   As dewes dropes ben wete,
As sterres ben in welkne and grases sour and swete.
Whoso loveth untrewe, his herte is selde sete.
Evere and o for my leef I am in grete thoght;
40   I thenke on hire that I ne see not ofte.

22. **dreccheth** afflicts
26. **hatheles** men, heroes; **hewes** servants
33. **fode** creature; **upon-lofte** alive
35. **fele sithe** many times, repeatedly
37. **welkne** sky
38. **untrewe** (one who is) untrue; **sete** content, satisfied

Litel wot it any man
How love Him hath i-bounde
That for us on the rode ran
4 And boghte us wyth His wounde.
The love of Him us hath i-maked sounde,
And i-cast the grimly gost to grounde.
Evere and o, nyght and day, He hath us in His thoght;
8 He nyl not lese that He so dere boghte.

He boghte us wyth His holy blood—
What sholde He don us more?
He is so meke, mylde, and good,
12 He nagulte not ther-fore.
That we han y-don I rede we rewen sore,
And crien evere to Jhesu, "Crist, thy ore!"
Evere and o, nyght and day, He hath us in His thoght;
16 He nyl not lese that He so dere boghte.

He saw His Fader so wonder wroth
Wyth man that was i-falle,
Wyth herte sore He seyde his oth
20 We sholde a-beyen alle.

Index 1922. MS. Harley 2253. (*EL XIII* No. 90.)
Unique text (but see *EL XIII*, pp. 235–37). *c.* 1320.

5. **sounde** healed, having salvation
6. **grimly gost** terrible (-looking) spirit, i.e., the Devil
8. **that** i.e., that which
12. **nagulte** = *ne agulte* did not sin
13. **that** i.e., (for) that which
17. **wonder wroth** wondrously angry
20. **a-beyen** pay the penalty for; redeem

His swete sone to Him gan clepe and calle,
And preyde He moot deyen for us alle.
Evere and o, nyght and day, He hath us in His thoght;
24 He nyl not lese that He so dere boghte.

He broghte us alle from the deeth
And dide us frendes dede.
Swete Jhesu of Nazareth,
28 Thou do us hevenes mede:
Upon the rode why nol we taken hede?
His grene wounde so grimly gonne blede.
Evere and o, nyght and day, He hath us in His thoght;
32 He nyl not lese that He so dere boghte.

His depe woundes bleden faste;
Of hem we oghte mynne.
He hath us out of helle i-cast,
36 I-broght us out of synne.
For love of us His wonges waxen thynne;
His herte blood He yaf for al mankynne.
Evere and o, nyght and day, He hath us in His thoght;
40 He nyl not lese that He so dere boghte.

29. **nol** = *ne wol* will not
30. **grene** fresh, bitter (*EL XIII* reads *greue*, *HL* reads *grene*);   **gonne** did
34. **mynne** remember, hold in mind
37. **wonges** cheeks

Al nyght by the rose, rose—
Al nyght by the rose I lay;
Durste I noght the rose stele,
4   And yet I bar the flour awey.

Index 194. MS. Rawlinson D. 913 [= Bodl. 13679]. (*SL XIV-XV* No. 17.)
Unique text. After 1300.

37

I am of Irelond,
And of the holy lond
Of Irelond.

Gode sire, preye I thee,
For-of Seint Charitee
Come and daunce wyth me
4   In Irelond.

Index 1008. MS. Rawlinson D. 913 [= Bodl. 13679]. (*SL XIV-XV* No. 15.)
Unique text. After 1300.

2. **For-of** for the sake of

38

Mayden in the moor lay—
In the moor lay—
   Seven-nyght fulle,
4   Seven-nyght fulle.
Mayden in the moor lay—
In the moor lay—
   Seven nyghtes fulle and a day.

8 Wel was hir mete.
What was hir mete?
   The prymerole and the—
   The prymerole and the—
12 Wel was hir mete.
What was hir mete?
   The prymerole and the vyolete.

Wel was hir drynke.
16 What was hir drynke?
   The colde water of the—
   The colde water of the—
Wel was hir drynke.
20 What was hir drynke?
   The colde water of the welle-spryng.

Index 3891 (*Supplement* 2037.5). MS. Rawlinson D. 913 [= Bodl. 13679]. (*SL XIV-XV* No. 18.)
Unique text. After 1300.

8. **Wel** good
10. **prymerole** primrose

Wel was hir bour.
What was hir bour?
24   The rede rose and the—
         The rede rose and the—
Wel was hir bour.
What was hir bour?
28   The rede rose and the lilye-flour.

39

Lullay, lullay, litel child, why wepest thou so sore?
Nedes most thou wepe, it was i-yarked thee yore—
Evere to lyve in sorwe, and sike and murne evere,
4 As thyne eldres dide er this, whil they alyve were.
   Lullay, lullay, litel child, child lullay, lullow,
   Into uncouth world i-comen so art thou.

Bestes and tho foules, the fisshes in the flood,
8 And ech shaft alyve i-maked of bon and blood—
Whan they comen to the world they don hem-selve
      som good,
Alle but the wrecche brolle that is of Adames blood.
   Lullay, lullay, litel child, to care thou art bimette;
12   Thou nost noght this worldes weild, bifore thee is i-set.

Child, if bitide that thou shalt thrive and thee,
Thenk thou wast i-fostred upon thy modres knee;
Evere have mynde in thyn herte of tho thynges three—
16 Whan thou comest, whan thou art, and what shal come
      of thee.
   Lullay, lullay, litel child, child lullay, lullay,
   Wyth sorwe thou cam into this world, wyth sorwe
      shalt wende awey.

Index 2025. MS. Harley 913. (*RL XIV* No. 28.)
Unique text. *c.* 1320.

2. **i-yarked** decreed, ordained
8. **shaft** creature
10. **brolle** child, offspring, wretch
11. **bimette** destined, consigned
12. **nost** = *ne wost*; **weild** meaning, signification (for MS. *wild*)
13. **thee** prosper
16. **Whan** whence

Ne trust thou to this world, it is thy ful fo—
20   The riche it maketh poure, the poure riche also;
In turneth wo to wele and eke wele to wo—
Ne trust no man to this world whil it turneth so.
    Lullay, lullay, litel child, the foot is in the wheel;
24   Thou nost whider turne to wo other wele.

Child, thou art a pilgrim in wikkednesse i-bore;
Thou wandrest in this false world—thou loke thee
    bifore.
Deeth shal come wyth a blast oute of a wel dim hore
28   Adames kyn doun to kaste, him-self hath i-don bifore.
    Lullay, lullay, litel child, so wo thee warp Adam
    In the lond of paradys thurgh wikkednesse of Satan.

Child, thou nart a pilgrim but an uncouth gest;
32   Thy dayes ben i-told, thy journeys ben i-cast.
Whider thou shalt wende, north other est,
Deeth thee shal bitide wyth bitter bale in brest.
    Lullay, lullay, litel child, this wo Adam thee wroght
36   Whan he of the appel eet, and Eve it him bitaughte.

20. *it* for MS. *he*
27. **wel dim hore** very dark mist, quite obscuring fog. See *OED* **haar.**
29. **warp** wove, prepared
31. **nart** = *ne art*
32. **journeys** days *or* day's journeys (?)
36. **bitaughte** gave

The lady Fortune is bothe frend and fo:
Of poure she maketh riche, or riche poure also;
She turneth wo al into wele, and wele al into wo.
4 Ne truste no man to this wele, the wheel it turneth so.

Index 3408. Camb. Univ. MS. Oo. 7. 32. (*RL XIV* No. 42.)
Several other texts, including one in French. *c.* 1325.

41

Hond by hond we shullen us take,
And joye and blisse shullen we make,
For the devel of helle man hath forsake,
And Goddes Sone is maked oure make.

A child is born amonges man,
And in that child was no wam;
That child is God, that child is man,
4   And in that child oure lyf bigan.

Synful man, be blithe and glad,
For youre mariage thy pees is grad
    Whan Crist was born!
8   Com to Crist—thy pees is grad;
For thee was his blood i-shad,
    That were forlorn.

Synful man, be blithe and bold,
12   For hevene is bothe boght and sold
    Everich a foot!
Com to Crist—thy pees is told;
For thee he yaf a hundredfold
16   His lyf to boot.

Index 29. MS. Bodley 26 (now Bodley 1871). (*RL XIV* No. 88.)
One other partial text. *c.* 1350.

2. **wam** blemish, stain
6. **pees is grad** peace is proclaimed
16. **to boot** as compensation, salvation

Lullay, lullay, litel child, child rest thee a throwe,
From heighe hider art thou sent wyth us to wonen lowe;
Poure and litel art thou made, uncouth and unknowe,
4 Pyne and wo to suffren heer for thyng that nas thyn owe.
   Lullay, lullay, litel child, sorwe myghte thou make;
   Thou are sent into this world, as thou were forsake.

Lullay, lullay, litel grome, kyng of alle thyng,
8 What I thenke of thy myschief me listeth wel litel synge;
But caren I may for sorwe, if love were in myn herte,
For swiche peynes as thou shalt dreyen were nevere non
      so smerte
   Lullay, lullay, litel child, wel myghte thou crie,
12   For-than thy body is bleik and blak, soon after shal
      ben drye.

Child, it is a wepyng dale that thou art comen in;
Thy poure cloutes it proven wel, thy bed made in the
      bynne;
Cold and hunger thou most tholen, as thou were geten
      in synne,
16 And after deyen on the tree for love of alle mankynne.

Index 2023. Advocates Lib. 18. 7. 21. (*RL XIV* No. 65.)
Unique text. *c.* 1370.

  1. **a throwe** for a time
  4. **nas** = *ne was*, replacing MS. *was*
  7. **grome** boy
10. **dreyen** suffer, endure
12. **bleik and blak** pallid and pale
14. **cloutes** clouts; (fragments of) cloth worn as clothing
15. **geten** begotten

Lullay, lullay, litel child, no wonder thogh thou care,
Thou art comen amonges hem that thy deeth shullen
    yare.

Lullay, lullay, litel child, for sorwe myghte thou grete;
20   The anguissh that thou suffren shalt shal don the blood
    to swete;
Naked, bounden shaltow ben, and sithen sore bete,
No thyng free upon thy body of pyne shal ben lete.
    Lullay, lullay, litel child, it is al for thy fo,
24   The harde bond of love-longyng that thee hath
    bounden so.

Lullay, lullay, litel child, litel child thyn ore!
It is al for oure owene gilt that thou art peyned sore.
But wolden we yet kynde ben and lyven after thy lore,
28   And leten synne for thy love, ne keptest thou no more.
    Lullay, lullay, litel child, softe sleep and faste,
    In sorwe endeth every love but thyn atte laste.

18. **yare** prepare, bring about
19. **grete** weep, cry
22. **lete** left, omitted
28. **ne keptest thou no more** you would not receive the blows (of punishment any more (for us), i.e., your suffering (in atonement for our sins)
would be at an end. *keptest* is preterite subjunctive; see *OED* **kep** and
keep (verb).

43

Whan men beth muriest at her mele
Wyth mete and drynke to maken hem glade,
Wyth worshipe and wyth worldly wele,
4   They ben so sete they conne not sade.
They han no deyntee for-to dele
Wyth thynges that ben devoutly made;
They wene her honour and her hele
8   Shal evere laste and nevere diffade.
But in her hertes I wolde they hadde,
When they gon richest men on array,
How soon that God hem may degrade,
12   And som tyme thenken on yesterday.

This day, as leef we mowen ben lighte,
Wyth alle the myrthes than men mowen vise,
To revel wyth thise burdes brighte,
16   Ech man gayest on his gise.
Atte laste it draweth to nyght,
That sleep moot maken his maistrise;
Whan that he hath i-kid his myght,
20   The morwe he busketh up to rise,—
Than al draweth him to fantasyse:
Wher he is bicomen can no man seye—

Index 3996. Vernon MS [= Bodl. 3938]. (*RL XIV* No. 101.)
One other text. *c.* 1370.

4. **sete** content; **sade** become serious, be concerned
5. **deyntee** fondness, pleasure
8. **diffade** fade, pass away
14. **vise** devise
16. **gise** style, fashion
18. **maistrise** mastery, domination
19. **i-kid** made known, manifested
20. **busketh** makes ready, prepares

And if they wiste they weren ful wyse—
24   For al is turned to yesterday.

    Whoso wolde thenken upon this
    Myghte fynd a good enchesoun why
    To preve this world, alwey, y-wis.
28   It nis but fantom and fairye:
    This erthly joye, this worldly blisse,
    Is but a fikel fantasye,
    For now it is and now it nis—
32   Ther may no man ther-inne affye;
    It chaungeth so ofte and so sodeynly,—
    To-day is heer, to-morwe awey.
    A siker ground he wole him gye,
36   I rede he thenke on yesterday.

    For ther nis non so strong in stour,
    From tyme that he ful waxen be,
    From that day forth everich an houre
40   Of his strengthe he leest a quantitee.
    Ne no burde so bright in bour
    Of thritty wynter, I ensure thee,
    That she ne shal faden as a flour—
44   Lite and lite lesen hir beautee.
    The sooth ye mowen your-selven ysee
    Ben youre eldres, in good fey;
    Whan ye ben grettest in youre degree
48   I rede ye thenken on yesterday.

16. **enchesoun** reason, cause
27. **preve** test
28. **fairye** illusion, magical contrivance
32. **affye** trust
35. **A siker ground** (If) on sure ground, on a certain foundation; **gye** (reflexive verb) conduct himself
37. **stour** battle
40. **leest** loses
44. **lite and lite** little by little

Nis non so fressh on foot to fare,
Ne non so faire on folde to fynde,
That they ne shullen on bere be broght ful bare.
52 This wrecched world nis but a wynd,
Ne non so stif to stynte ne stare,
Ne non so bold beres to bynde
That he nath warnynges to be war.
56 For God is so curteis and so kynde,
Bihold the lame, the bedrede, the blynde,
That bidde you be war while that ye may:
They maken a mirour to your mynde
60 To see the shap of yesterday.

The lyf that any man shal lede
Beth certeyn dayes atte laste;
Than moste our terme shorte nedes,
64 Be oon day comen another is passed.
Heer-of if we wolden take good hede
And in our hertes acountes caste,
Day by day, wythouten drede,
68 Toward our ende we drawen ful faste;
Than shullen oure bodies in erthe be thrast,
Oure careynes couched under cley.
Heer-of we oghte ben sore agast,
72 If we wolden thenke on yesterday.

49. **non . . . on foot to fare** no one to go on foot, i.e., anyone at all
50. **fold** earth
51. **bere** bier
53. **stif** strong, valiant
55. **nath** = *ne hath*
58. **may** = *mowen*
63. **moste oure terme shorte nedes** must our term (time of life) necessarily shorten
65. *if* for MS. *and* here and in l. 72
69. **thrast** thrust, put
70. **careynes** dead bodies

70

Salomon seyde, in his poesye,
He holdeth wel bettre wyth an hound
That is likyng and joly,
76 And of siknesse hol and sound,
Thanne be a leoun thogh he lie
Cold and deed upon the grounde.
Wher-of serveth his victorie,
80 That was so stif in ech a stounde?
The moste fool, I herde respounde,
Is wyser whil he lyven may,
Thanne he that hadde a thousand pound
84 And was buried yesterday.

Socrates seyth a word ful wys:
It were wel bettre for-to see
A man that now parteth and deyes
88 Thanne a feste of realtee.
The feste wol maken his flessh to rise,
And drawe his herte to vanytee;
The body that on the bere lies
92 Sheweth the same that we shullen be.
That fereful fit may no man flee,
Ne wyth no wyles wynne it awey:
Ther-fore among al jolitee
96 Som tyme thenk on yesterday.

But yet me merveileth over al
That God lett many man croke and elde,
Whan myght and strengthe is from hem falle,

77. **leoun** lion
81. **respounde** answer
87. **parteth** departs; **deyes** = *deyeth*
88. **feste of realtee** sumptuous, splendid feast
91. **lies** = *lieth*
93. **fit** terrible or violent experience
98. **croke** become bent, crooked

100   That they mowen not hem-selven a-welde;
And now thise beggars most principal
That good ne profit mowen non yelde.
To this purpose answere I shal
104   Why God sente swiche men boot and belde:
Crist that made bothe flour and feeld
Lett swiche men lyven, for-sothe to seye,
Whan a yong man on hem bihelde
108   Sholde see the shap of yesterday.

Another skile ther is for-why
That God lett swiche men lyven so longe:
For they ben treacle and remedye
112   For synfulle men that han don wronge.
In hem the sevene dedes of mercy
A man may fulfille among,
And also thise proude men mowen ther-by
116   A faire mirour underfonge.
For ther nis no so stif ne strong,
Ne no lady so stout ne gay,—
Bihold what over her hed can honge,
120   And som tyme thenk on yesterday.

I have wist, sith I coude mynne,
That children han by candel light
Her shadwe on the wal i-seen
124   And ronne ther-after al the nyght.
Bisy aboute they han ben
To cacchen it wyth al her myght;

100. **a-welde** control, maintain rule
104. **boot and belde** relief and comfort
109. **skile** reason, argument
111. **treacle** salve, remedy
116. **underfonge** take
118. *so* not in MS.
121. **mynne** remember

And whan they cacchen it best wolden wene,
128 Sannest it schet out of her sight.
The shadwe cacchen they ne myghte,
For no lynes that they coude leye.
This shadwe I may likne aright
132 To this world and yesterday.

Into this world whan we ben broght
We shullen be tempt to covetise,
And al thy wit shal be thurgh-soght
136 To more good thanne thou mowe suffise.
Whan thou thenkest best in thy thoght
On richesse for-to regne and rise,
Al thy travaile turneth to noght,
140 For sodeynly on deeth thou deyes.
Thy lyf thou hast i-lad wyth lyes,
So this world gan thee bitraye:
Ther-fore I rede thou this despise
144 And som tyme thenke on yesterday.

Man, if thy neighebore thee manace,
Other to kille or to bete,
I knowe me siker in the cas
148 That thou wolt drede thy neighebores threte,
And nevere a day thy dore to passe
Wythouten siker defence and grete,
And ben purveied in ech a place
152 Of sikernesse and help to gete.

128. **Sannest** suddenly, quickly; **schet** vanishes
130. **lynes** lines, cords (for catching birds)
134. **covetise** covetousness, avarice
135. **thurgh-soght** thoroughly penetrated, suffused
140. **deyes** = *deyest*
141. **lyes** falsehood
145. **manace** menace, threaten
146. **other** either
147. **siker in the cas** assuredly in that circumstance

Thyn enemy woltow not forgete
But ay be aferd of his affray.
Ensaumple heer-of I wol thee trete
156   To maken thee thenke of yesterday.

Wel thou wost wythouten faile
That deeth hath manaced thee to deye,
But whan that he wol thee assaile,
160   That wost thou not, ne nevere most spye.
If thou wolt don by my counseil,
Wyth siker defence be ay redy;
For siker defence in this bataile
164   Is clene lyf, parfit, and trie.
Put thy trust in Goddes mercy,
It is the best at al assay,
And evere among thou thee en-nuye
168   Into this world and yesterday.

Som men seyn that deeth is a theef
And al unwarned wol on hem stele;
And I seye nay, and make a preef
172   That deeth is stedefast, trewe, and lele,
And warneth ech man of his greef
That he wol oon day wyth him dele.
The lyf that is to you so leef
176   He wol you reve, and eke youre hele—
Thise poyntes may no man him repele;
He cometh so boldely to pike his pray,
Whan men beth muriest at her mele,—
180   I rede ye thenken on yesterday.

155. **ensaumple** instance; **trete** discuss; *thee* for MS. ȝou (also in 156)
164. **trie** excellent
167. **en-nuye** become weary (reflexive verb)
171. **preef** proof
172. **lele** loyal, faithful
178. **pike** get, pick out, plunder

44

My cares comen evere anewe—
   A! dere God, no boot ther nis,
For I am holden for untrewe
4   Wythouten gilt, so have I blisse.

To be trewe woned I was
   In any thyng I myghte don;
I thonked God his grete grace:
8   Now it is I may noght don.

Index 2231. MS. Douce 381 [= Bodl. 21956]. (*SL XIV-XV* No. 150.)
With music. Unique text. *c.* 1390

5. **woned** accustomed

45

"A! Sone, tak hede to me whos sone thou wast
And set me wyth thee upon thy cros—
Me heer to leve and thee hennes thus go:
4   It is to me greet care and endeles wo.
Stynt now, Sone, to be hard to thy moder,
Thou that were ever goodly to al othere."

"Stynt now, Moder, and weep namore;
8   Thy sorwe and thy disese greve me ful sore.
Thou knowest that in thee I took mannes kynde,
In this for mannes synne to be thus pyned.
But now glad, Moder, and have in thy thoght
12   That mannes hele is founde that I have soght.
Thou shalt not now care what thou shalt don,
Lo! John thy cosyn shal be thy sone."

Index 14. Balliol Coll. Oxf. MS. 149. (*RL XIV* No. 128.)
One other text. *c.* 1390.

12. **hele** salvation
13. **care** have concern, solicitude

46

Marie moder, wel thee be!
Marie mayden, thenk on me!
Moder and mayden was nevere non
4   Togidre, lady, but thou allone.

Marie moder, mayden clene,
Shild me, lady, from sorwe and tene;
Marie, out of synne help thou me,
8   And out of dette for charitee.

Marie, for thy joyes five,
Help me to lyve in clene lyve;
For the teres thou lette under the rode,
12   Sende me grace of lyves fode

Wher-wyth I may me clothe and fede,
And in trouthe my lyf lede.
Help me, lady, and alle myne,
16   And shild us alle from helle-pyne.

Shild me, lady, from vilanye,
And from alle wikked companye;
Shild me, lady, from wikked shame,
20   And from alle wikked fame.

Index 2119. MS. Rawlinson liturgical g.2 [= Bodl. 15834]. (*RL XIV* No. 122.)

More than fifty other texts extant. Before 1400.

6. **tene** suffering, grief; *lady* not in MS.
11. **lette** shed
12. **fode** sustenance, livelihood
17. **vilanye** shameful, ignominious conduct; villainy

Swete lady, thou me were
That the feend noght me dere;
Bothe by day and by nyght
24   Help me, lady, wyth thy right.

For my frendes I bidde thee
That they mowen amended be,
Bothe to soule and to lyf,
28   Marie, for thy joyes five.

For my fo-men I bidde also
That they mowen heer so do
That they in wraththe heighe ne deye,
32   Swete lady, I thee preye.

They that ben in gode lyve,
Marie, for thy joyes five,
Swete lady, ther-inne hem holde,
36   Bothe the yonge and the olde.

And tho that ben in deedly synne,
Ne lat hem nevere deye ther-inne;
Marie, for thy joyes alle,
40   Lat hem nevere in helle falle.

Swete lady, thou hem rede
That they amenden of her mysdede;
Biseech thy Sone, hevenes kyng
44   That He me graunte good endyng;

And sende me, as He wel may,
Shrift and housel at myn endyng-day;
And that we mowen thider wende
48   Ther joye is wythouten ende. Amen. Amen.

21. were protect   **22. dere** injure   **37. tho** not in MS.

47

Wyth a gerlond of thornes kene
Myn hed was crouned, and that was sene;
SUPERBIA
The stremes of blood renne by my cheke:
4 Thou proude man, lerne to be meke.

Whan thou are wroth and woldest take wreche,
Kepe wel the lore that I thee teche;
IRA
Thurgh my right hond the nayle goth:
8 Foryeve ther-fore and be not wroth.

Wyth a spere sharp and gril
Myn herte was wounded, wyth my wyl,
INUIDIA
For love of man that was me dere:
12 Envious man, of love thou lere.

Ris up, Lust, out of thy bed,
Thenk on my feet that are for-bledde
ACCIDIA
And harde nayled upon a tree:
16 Thenk on, man, this was for thee.

Index 4185. Camb. Univ. Lib. Ff. 5.48. (Henry A. Person, *Cambridge Middle English Lyrics*, rev. ed., 1962, No. 8.)

One other text. *c.* 1400.

Beside each of the first seven stanzas in the manuscript is a Latin tag to identify one of the seven deadly sins: **Superbia** Pride, **Ira** Wrath, **Inuidia** Envy, **Accidia** Sloth, **Auaricia** Avarice, **Gula** Gluttony, and **Luxuria** Lechery. **Ihesuc** Jesus

5. **wreche** vengeance
9. **gril** harsh, cruel
13. **Lust** bodily pleasure. The other text (*RL XIV* No. 127) reads *vnlust* sluggard.

Thurgh my left hond the nayle was dryven—
Thenk ther-on, if thou wylle lyven;

AUARICIA

And worship God wyth almes-dede
20   That at thy deying hevene may be thy mede.

In alle my peynes I suffred on rode
Man yaf me drynke no thyng gode—

GULA

Eisel and galle for-to drynke:
24   Glotoun, ther-on evere thou thenk.

Of a mayden I was born
To save the folk that weren forlorn;

LUXURIA

Al my body was beten for synne:
28   Lechour, ther-fore I rede thee blynne.

I was beten for thy sake—
Synne thou leve and shrift thou tak;

IHESUC

Forsak thy synne and love me,
32   Amend thee, and I foryeve thee.

17. *left* for MS. *right*
23. **Eisel** vinegar

48

Esto memor mortis iam porta sit omnibus ortis
Sepe sibi iuuenes accipit ante senes.

Sith al that in this world hath ben *in rerum natura,*
Or in this wide world was seen *in humana cura,*
Alle shullen passe wythouten ween *via mortis dura;*
4   God graunte that mannes soule ben clene *penas non*
        passura.
  Whan thou leeste wenest, *veniet mors te superare:*
  Thus thy grave greveth, *ergo mortis memorare.*

Vnde vir extolleris, thou shalt be wormes mete,
8 *Qui quamdiu vixeris* thy synnes wolde thou not lete;
Quamuis diues fueris and of power greet,
Cum morte percuteris help myghte thou non gete.
  Si diues fias do thy-self good, man, wyth thyne hondes;
12 *Post necis ergo uias* ful fewe wol lose thee of thy bondes.

Index 3122. Camb. Univ. MS. Ee. 6. 29. (*RL XIV* No. 135.)
Five other texts. *c.* 1400.

> Be mindful of death: now there is a gate for all men born; often it takes to itself young men before old. (Translations of the remaining Latin passages are given without repeating the original half-line.)

1. in the nature of things, i.e., in the created world
2. in human care
3. **ween** doubt; along the hard way of death
4. (so as) not to suffer punishment
5. **leeste wenest** least expect; death will come to overwhelm you
6. **greveth** (?) afflicts, (?) inters; therefore remember death
7. when you, as a man, will be carried away, *or* when, O man, you are (to be) carried away
8. who as long as you will live
9. although you will have been rich
10. when you will be shattered by death
11. if you would be rich
12. after the ways of death; **lose** loosen, free

This oghte wel to felle thy pride, *quod es moriturus;*
Thou knowest neither tyme ne tide *qua es decessurus.*
Wormes shullen ete thy bak and side, *inde sis securus:*
16   As thou hast wroght in this world wide *sic es recepturus.*
    Thus deeth thee ledeth, *terre tumilo quasi nudum;*
    Deeth no man dredeth, *mors terminat hiccine ludum.*

    Nam nulli vult parcere deeth that is un-dere,
20   *Pro argenti munere,* ne for no faire preyere;
    Sed dum rapit propere, he chaungeth ech mannes chere,
    In peccati scelere if he be founden heer.
    Set cum dampnatis helle to thy mede thou wynnest,
24   That nevere blynneth *pro peccatis sceleratis.*

    Whan I thenke upon my deeth, *tunc sum contristatus,*
    And waxe as hevy as any leed *meos ob reatus;*
    Deeth turneth into wrecchedhede *viros magni status,*
28   Than may no thyng stonde in stede *mundi dominatus.*
    Wyth ful bare bones *mundi rebus cariturus,*
    Thus from thise wones *transit numquam rediturus.*

13. **felle** destroy, put down; the fact that you are going to die
14. at which you are going to descend
15. of that you may be sure
16. so you are going to receive
17. in a mound of earth as if naked
18. death ends the game at this point
19. for he is willing to spare no one; **un-dere** hated, feared
20. for a gift of money
21. while he snatches you quickly away; **chere** appearance
22. in (an evil) deed of sin
23. but with the damned
24. for thy wicked sins
25. then I am sorrowful
26. **leed** lead; on account of my thoughts
27. **wrecchedhede** (state of) wretchedness; men of high standing
28. the lordship (rule) of the world
29. to lack (be absent from) the world
30. **wones** dwellings, abodes; you pass never to return

Caro vermis ferculum, thenk on the pynes of helle;
32 *Mors habet spiculum* that smyteth man ful felle;
Te ponet ad tumilum til domes-day to dwelle.
Hic relinquis seculum; ther nis noght elles to telle.
  Mors cito cuncta rapit; ther-fore, man, thenk on thy
    werkes.
36 Thus seyn thise clerkes: *mors cito cuncta rapit.*

God that deyde on the tree *pro nostra salute,*
And aros after dayes three *diuina uirtute,*
Yif us grace synne to flee *stante iuuentute,*
40 On domes-day that we mowen see *vultum tuum tute.*
  Dolful deeth drede I thee, *veniet quia nescio quando:*
  Be redy ther-fore, I warne thee, *de te peccata fugando.*

31. flesh is a worm's dish
32. death has a dart (arrow); **felle** cruelly, destructively
33. he will place you in the tomb
34. you leave, here, the world (behind)
35. death carries all things quickly off
36. death carries all things quickly off
37. for our salvation
38. by divine power
39. while youth lasts
40. thy countenance safely
41. because he will come I know not when
42. by putting thy sins to flight from thee

49

In a tabernacle of a tour,
As I stood musyng on the mone,
A crouned quene, most of honour,
4 Appered in gostly sight ful soon.
She made compleynte thus by hir oon
For mannes soule was wrapped in wo:
"I may not leve mankynde allone
8   *Quia amore langueo.*

"I longe for love of man my brother;
I am his vocate to voide his vice,
I am his moder—I can non other—
12 Why sholde I my dere child despise?
If he me wrathe in diverse wyse,
Thurgh flesshes freeltee falle me fro,
Yet moot we rewe him til he rise,
16   *Quia amore langueo.*

"I bidde, I bide in greet longynge;
I love, I loke whan man wol crave;
I pleyne for pitee of peynynge.
20 Wolde he axe mercy he sholde it have.
Sey to me, soule, and I shal save;
Bid me, my child, and I shal go;

Index 1460. MS. Douce 322. (*RL XIV* No. 132.)
Eight other texts of varying extent. *c.* 1400.

1. **tabernacle** = (?) niche (in a wall), covered seat
8. **Quia amore langueo** because I languish (swoon) with love
10. **vocate** advocate, intercessor; **voide** expel, remove
13. **If he me wrathe** If he should provoke me to anger
14. **freeltee** frailty. *Thurgh* for MS. *Though*
15. *me* (from other MSS.) replacing *we*

Thou preydest me nevere but my Sone foryaf,—
24 *Quia amore langueo.*

"O wrecche in the world, I loke on thee;
I see thy trespas day by day
Wyth lechery ayeins my chastitee,
28 Wyth pride ayeins my poure array.
My love abideth, thyn is awey;
My love thee calleth, thou stelest me fro;
Sewe to me synner, I thee preye,
32 *Quia amore langueo.*

"Moder of mercy I was for thee made.
Who nedeth it but thou allone?
To gete thee grace I am more gladde
36 Thanne thou to axe it—why woltow non?
Whan seyde I nay, tel me, to oon?
For sothe, nevere yet to freend ne fo.
Whan thou axest noght, than make I mone,
40 *Quia amore langueo.*

"I seche thee in wele and wrecchednesse,
I seche thee in richesse and povertee.
Thou man, bihold wher thy moder is!
44 Why lovest thou me not sith I love thee?
Synful or sory, how evere thou be,
So welcome to me ther are no mo.
I am thy suster; right trust on me,—
48 *Quia amore langueo.*

31. **Sewe** (from another MS.) petition, replacing MS. *shewe*

"My child is outlawed for thy synne,
My child is beten for thy trespas;
Yet priketh myn herte that so nigh my kyn
52   Sholde be disesed. —O Sone, allas!
Thou art his brother! Thy moder I was—
Thou soukedest my pappe! Thou lovedest man so,
Thou deydest for him! Myn herte he has,
56   *Quia amore langueo.*

"Man, leve thy synne than for my sake!
Why sholde I yeve thee that thou not wolde?
And yet if thou synne, som preyere tak
60   Or trust in me as I have tolde.
Am not I thy moder called?
Why sholdest thou flee? I love thee, lo!
I am thy freend, thy help, bihold!
64   *Quia amore langueo.*

"Now, Sone," she seyde, "woltow seye nay
Whan man wolde mende him of his mys?
Thou lette me nevere in vayne yet preye.—
68   Than, synful man, see thou to this,
What day thou comest, welcome thou is
This hundreth yeer, if thou were me fro;
I take thee ful fayne, I clyppe, I kisse,
72   *Quia amore langueo.*

---

50. *My child is beten for thy trespas* from another MS., replacing *Mankind ys bette for hys trespasse*
53. *Thy* (from another MS.) replacing *hys*
58. **wolde** = woldest
62. *Why sholdest thou flee* (from other MSS.) replacing *Why shulde I flee the*
63. *thy help* (from another MS.) replacing *I helpe*
66. **mys** wrongdoing, offenses

"Now wol I sitte and seye namore,
Leve and loke wyth greet longynge;
Whan a man wol calle I wol restore.
76 I love to save him, he is myn ofsprynge;
No wonder if myn herte on him hynge.
He was my neighebore—what may I do?
For him hadde I this worshipynge,
80   And therefore *amore langueo*.

"Why was I crouned and made a quene?
Why was I called of mercy the welle?
Why sholde an erthly womman ben
84 So heighe in hevene above aungel?
For thee, mankynde, the trouthe I telle!
Thou axe me help and I shal do
That I was ordeyned—kepe thee from helle,
88   *Quia amore langueo*.

"Now, man, have mynde on me for evere;
Loke on thy love thus languisshyng;
Lete us nevere from other dissevere.
92 Myn help is thyn owene, creep under my wyng;
Thy suster is a quene, thy brother a kyng;
This heritage is tailed, soon com ther-to!
Tak me for thy wyf and lerne to synge,
96   *Quia amore langueo*."

74. **Leve and loke** cease and wait (expectantly)
77. **hynge** hang
87. **that** i.e., that which
91. **dissevere** separate
94. **tailed** entailed
95. *wyf.* Another MS. reads *moder*

50

In the vale of resteles mynde
I soghte in mountayne and in meed
Trustyng a trew-love for-to fynde.
4   Upon an hil than took I hede;
A vois I herde (and neer I yede)
In greet dolour compleynyng tho:
"See, dere soule, my sides blede,
8   *Quia amore langueo.*"

Upon this mount I fond a tree;
Under this tree a man sittyng.
From hed to foot wounded was he,
12 His herte blood I saw bledyng;
A seemly man to ben a kyng,
A gracious face to loke unto.
I axed him how he hadde peynyng:
16 He seyde, "*Quia amore langueo.*

"I am trewe-love that fals was nevere;
My suster, mannes soule, I lovede hire thus:
Bicause I wolde on no wyse dissevere
20 I lefte my kyngdom glorious;

Index 1463. Camb. Univ. Lib. Hh. 4.12, with variants from Lambeth
MS. 853. (Both in F. J. Furnivall, ed., *Political, Religious, and
Love Poems*, EETS o.s. 15 [1866].)
Two texts. *c.* 1430.

5. **yede** went, walked
8. **Quia amore langueo** because I languish (swoon) with love. (See the
Song of Solomon.)
19. **dissevere** separate

I purveiede hire a place ful precious.
She flitte, I folwed, I lovede hire so
That I suffred thise peynes piteous,
24 *Quia amore langueo.*

"My faire love and my spouse brighte
I savede hire from betyng and she hath me bette;
I clothede hire in grace and hevenly light:
28 This blody sherte she hath on me set.
For longyng love I wol not lete.
Swete strokes ben thise, lo!
I have loved evere as I hette,
32 *Quia amore langueo.*

"I crounede hire wyth blisse and she me wyth thorn;
I ledde hire to chambre and she me to deye;
I broghte hire to worshipe and she me to scorn:
36 I dide hire reverence and she me vilanye.
To love that loveth is no maistrye;
Hir hate made nevere my love hir fo.
Axe than no more questiouns why,
40 But *quia amore langueo.*

"Loke unto myne hondes, man!
Thise gloves were yeven me whan I hire soghte.
They ben not white, but rede and wan;
44 Enbrouded wyth blood my spouse hem boghte.

21. **purveiede** provided
28. **sherte** shirt, from Lambeth MS., replacing *surcote*
29. **lete** cease
31. **hette** promised; *evere* replaces MS. *ouer*
36. **vilanye** shameful, ignominious conduct, villainy
37. **that** i.e., that one who
43. **wan** dark

They wol not offe; I leve hem noght;
I wowe hire wyth hem wher-evere she go.
Thise hondes ful freendly for hire foghte,
48   *Quia amore langueo.*

"Merveil not, man, thogh I sitte stille,—
My love hath shod me wonder streyte:
She bokeled my feet, as was hir wylle,
52   Wyth sharpe nayles—wel thou mayst waite.
In my love was never disceite,
For alle my membres I have opened hire to;
My body I made hir hertes baite,
56   *Quia amore langueo.*

"In my side I have made hir neste.
Loke in, how wide a wounde is heer:
This is hir chambre, heer shal she reste,
60   That she and I mowen slepe in fere.
Heer may she wasshe if any filthe were;
Heer is socour for al hir wo.
Come if she wyl, she shal have chere,
64   *Quia amore langueo.*

"I wol abide til she be redy;
I wol to hire sende er she seye nay;
If she be reccheles I wol be redy,
68   If she be daungerous I wol hire preye;

---

50. **wonder streyte** very closely, tightly
52. **waite** look, observe
55. **baite** lure, enticement
58. *Loke in*, omitting *me*, as in Lambeth MS.
60. **in fere** together, as companions
67. **reccheles** without care, negligent
68. **daungerous** disdainful

If she do wepe than bidde I nay:
Myne armes ben sprad to clyppe hire to.
Cry ones 'I come,' now, soule, assay,
72   *Quia amore langueo.*

"I sitte on an hil for to see fer;
I loke to the vale my spouse to see.
Now renneth she aweyward, now cometh she nere,
76   Yet from myn eye-sight she may not be.
Som wayte her pray to make hire flee,
I renne to-fore to fleme hir fo.
Retourn, my soule, ageyn to me,
80   *Quia amore langueo.*

"My swete spouse, lat us go pleye—
Apples ben ripe in my gardyn;
I shal thee clothe in newe array,
84   Thy mete shal be milk, hony, and wyne.
Now, dere soule, lete us go dyne—
Thy sustenaunce is in my scrippe, lo!
Tary not now, faire spouse myn,
88   *Quia amore langueo.*

70. **clyppe** clasp
71. **ones** once
74. *to see*, from Lambeth MS., replacing *I see*
78. **fleme** put to flight, from Lambeth MS., replacing *chastise*
79. *Retourn*, from Lambeth MS., replacing *recouer*
81. *lat us*, from Lambeth MS., replacing *will we*
83. *thee clothe*, from Lambeth MS., replacing *clothe the*
86. **scrippe** bag, wallet (for food)

"If thou be foule I shal make thee clene;
If thou be sik I shal thee hele;
If thou aught murne I shal thee mene.
92 Spouse, why wyltow not wyth me dele?
Thou founde nevere love so lele.
What wyltow, soule, that I shal do?
I may of unkyndnesse thee appele,
96   *Quia amore langueo.*

"What shal I do now wyth my spouse?
Abide I wol hir gentilnesse.
Wolde she loke ones out of hir hous
100 Of flesshly affecciouns and unclennesse,
Hir bed is made, hir bolster is in blisse,
Hir chambre is chosen, swiche are no mo.
Loke out at the wyndowes of kyndenesse,
104   *Quia amore langueo.*

"My spouse is in chambre—hold thy pees!
Make no noise, but lat hire slepe.
My babe shal suffre no disese;
108 I may not here my dere child wepe;
For wyth my pappe I shal hire kepe.
No wonder thogh I tende hire to,
This hole in my side hadde nevere ben so depe,
112   But *quia amore langueo.*

89. *thee* not in MS.
91. **mene** pity; *thee mene*, from Lambeth MS., replacing *be-mene*
93. **lele** loyal, faithful
95. **appele** accuse
100. **flesshly** worldly; carnal-minded
105–20. The order of this stanza and the next one is reversed, following
    Lambeth MS.

"Longe and love thou nevere so heighe,
Yet is my love more thanne thyn may be;
Thou gladdest, thou wepest, I sitte thee by;
116 Yet myghte thou, spouse, loke ones at me.
Spouse, sholde I alwey fede thee
Wyth childes mete? Nay, love, not so!
I wol preve thy love wyth adversitee,
120   *Quia amore langueo.*

"Wax not wery, myn owene dere wyf!
What mede is ay to lyve in confort?
For in tribulacioun I regne more rife
124 Ofter tymes thanne in desport;
In welthe, in wo, evere I supporte.
Than, dere soule, go nevere me fro—
Thy mede is marked, whan thou art mort
   In blisse; *quia amore langueo.*"

119. **preve** test; *I wol preve thy love,* from Lambeth MS., replacing *I pray the love*
124. **desport** amusement, entertainment
127. **mort** dead

51

Deo gracias anglia,
Redde pro victoria.

Oure kyng went forth to Normandy
Wyth grace and myght of chivalry;
Ther God for him wroghte merveilously,
4   Wherfor Englond may calle and crie:
    "*Deo gracias!*"

He sette a sege, the soth for-to seye,
To Harflu toun wyth royal array;
8   That toun he wan and made affray
That Fraunce shal rewe til domesday.
    Deo gracias!

Than went oure kyng wyth al his ost
12 Thurgh Fraunce, for al the Frenshe bost;
He spared no drede of leest ne most
Til he cam to Agincourt cost.
    Deo gracias!

Index 2716. MS. Arch. Selden B. 26 [= Bodl. 3340]. (*HP XIV-XV* No. 32.)

One other version. "The Agincourt Carol," on the occasion of Henry V's famous victory at Agincourt; perhaps used in celebrations upon Henry's return to London. With music. 1415.

    Deo . . . victoria Return thanks to God, England, for victory
6. **He sette a sege** he lay siege
7. **To Harflu toun** before Harfleur; **array** display of military force
8. **affray** disturbance, terror (caused by attack or fighting)
11. **ost** (military) host, army
12. **bost** boast, vaunt, threatening
13. **He spared no drede** he shunned no dreaded things, he did not keep clear of (things of) danger
14. **cost** district, bordering area

16   Than for sothe that knight comly
In Agincourt feeld he faught manly;
Thurgh grace of God moste myghty
He hadde bothe the feeld and the victorie.
20   *Deo gracias!*

Ther dukes and erles, lord and baroun,
Were take and slayn, and that wel soon;
And som were led in-to Londoun
24   Wyth joye and myrthe and greet renoun.
Deo gracias!

Now gracious God he save oure kyng,
His peple, and alle his wel-wyllyng;
28   Yeve him good lyf and good endyng,
That we wyth myrthe mowe saufly synge:
"*Deo gracias!*"

24. **renoun** display, distinction
27. **wel-wyllyng** well wishers, i.e., friends

52

Querela diuina

> O Man unkynde, have in mynde,
> > My peynes smerte!
> Bihold and see that is for thee
> 4   Perced myn herte.
>
> And yet I wolde, er-than thou sholde
> > Thy soule forsake,
> On cros wyth peyne sharp deeth ageyn
> 8   For thy love take.
>
> For which I axe non other taske
> > But love ageyn.
> Me than to love alle thynges above
> 12   Thou oghte ben fayn.

Responsio humana

> O Lord, right dere, thy wordes I here
> > Wyth herte ful sore;
> Ther-fore from synne I hope to blynne
> 16   And greve no more.

Index 2504. B. M. Addit. MS. 37049. (*RL XV* No. 108.)
Two other texts, one of which transcribes an inscription in Almondbury
Church, Yorkshire. *c.* 1430.

5. **er-than** before, sooner; rather than
16. **greve** cause pain (to)

But in this cas now helpe thy grace
 My freelnesse,
That I may evere don thy plesure
20 Wyth lastyngnesse.

This grace to gete, thy modres eke,
 Evere be proon,
That we mowen alle into thy halle
24 Wyth joye come soon. Amen.

18. **freelnesse** frailness, frailty
22. **proon** eager, prone, ready (in mind)

53

Adam lay i-bounde,
　　Bounden in a bond;
Foure thousand wynter
4　　Thoghte he not to longe.
And al was for an appel,
　　An appel that he took,
As clerkes fynden writen
8　　In here book.

Ne hadde the appel take ben,
　　The appel take ben,
Ne hadde nevere oure lady
12　　A ben hevenes quene.
Blessed by the tyme
　　That appel take was,—
Ther-fore we mowen synge
16　　*"Deo gracias."*

Index 117. MS. Sloane 2593. (*RL XV* No. 83.)
Unique text. *c.* 1430

54

I syng of a mayden that is makeles:
Kyng of alle kynges to hir sone she ches.

He cam also stille ther his moder was
4 As dewe in Aprill that falleth on the gras.

He cam also stille to his modres bour
As dewe in Aprill that falleth on the flour.

He cam also stille ther his moder lay
8 As dewe in Aprill that falleth on the spray.

Moder and mayden was nevere non but she:
Wel may swich a lady Goddes moder be.

Index 1367. MS. Sloane 2593. (*RL XV* No. 81.)
Unique text. *c.* 1430.

2. **ches** chose
3. **also stille** as silently, as gently; **ther** (there) where

55

Now bithenk thee, gentilman,
How Adam dalf and Eve span.

In the vale of Abraham
Crist him-self he made Adam,
And of his ryb a faire womman;
4   And thus this seemly world bigan.

"Com, Adam, and thou shalt see
The blisse of paradys that is so free;
Ther-inne stant an appel-tree—
8   Leef and fruyt growen ther-on.

"Adam, if thou this appel ete,
Alle thise joyes thou shalt foryete
And the peynes of helle gete."
12   Thus God him-self warned Adam.

Whan God was from Adam gon,
Soon after cam the feend anon—
A fals traitour he was oon.
16   He took the tree and crepte ther-on.

Index 1568. MS. Sloane 2593. (*EEC* No. 336.)
Unique text. *c.* 1430.

    Adam dalf and Eve span Adam labored (by digging) and Eve spun.
This is a formula put to several uses over several generations; cf. *OED*
delve.
10. **foryete** lose, give up

100

"What eyleth thee, Adam, art thou wood?
Thy Lord hath taught thee litel good!
He wolde not thou understood
20   Of the wyttes that he can.

"Tak the appel offe the tree
And ete ther-of, I bidde thee,
And alle thise joyes thou shalt see;
24   From thee he shal hiden non."

Whan Adam hadde that appel ete,
Alle thise joyes weren foryete;
Non word more myghte he speke.
28   He stood as naked as a ston.

Than cam an aungel wyth a swerd
And drof Adam into a desert;
Ther was Adam sore aferd,
32   For labour coude he werke non.

20. **wyttes** (things of) knowledge, wisdom

56

I have a yong suster
    Fer biyonde the see;
    Many ben the drueries
4   That she sente me.

She sente me the chery
    Wythouten any ston,
And so she dide the dowve
8   Wythouten any bon.

She sente me the brere
    Wythouten any rynde,
She bad me love my lemman
12   Wythouten longynge.

How sholde any chery
    Ben wythouten ston?
And how sholde any dowve
16   Ben wythouten bon?

How sholde any brere
    Ben wythouten rynde?
How sholde I love my lemman
20   Wythouten longynge?

Index 1303. MS. Sloane 2593. (*SL XIV-XV* No. 45.)
Unique text, but similar paradoxes are common. *c.* 1430.

 3. **drueries** presents, keepsakes; (?) love tokens
 9. **brere** (stock of) a wild rose
10. **rynde** bark (of a plant)
19. *sholde I love* for MS. *xuld love*

Whan the chery was a flour,
  Than hadde it non ston;
Whan the dowve was an ey,
24   Than hadde it non bon.

Whan the brere was unbred,
  Than hadde it non rynde;
Whan the mayden hath that she loveth,
28   She is wythouten longynge.

23. **ey** egg
25. **unbred** unborn, i.e., a seed

57

How! hey! It is non lees,
I dar not seyn whan she seyth "Pees!"

Yonge men, I warne you everichoon,
Elde wyves taketh ye non—
For I my-self have oon at hom:
4   I dar not seyn whan she seyth "Pees!"

Whan I come from the plough at noon,
In a riven dissh my mete is don;
I dar not axen oure dame a spoon—
8   I dar not seyn whan she seyth "Pees!"

If I axe oure dame breed,
She taketh a staf and breketh myn hed,
And doth me rennen under the bed.
12   I dar not seyn whan she seyth "Pees!"

If I axe oure dame flessh,
She breketh myn hed with a dissh:
"Boy, thou art not worth a rissh!"
16   I dar not seyn whan she seyth "Pees!"

If I axe oure dame chese,
"Boy," she seyth, al at ese,
"Thou are not worth half a pese!"
20   I dar not seyn whan she seyth "Pees!"

Index 4279. MS. Sloane 2593. (*SL XIV-XV* No. 43.)
Unique text. *c.* 1430.

    lees lie, falsehood; **seyn** say (anything), i.e., speak
15. **Boy** is used contemptuously in addressing a person; **rissh** (stalk of a)
    rush, "not worth a straw"
19. **pese** pea, hence "you are worthless" (cf. l. 15)

58

Synge we alle and seye we thus:
Gramercy, myn owene purs.

When I have in my purs ynough,
I may have bothe hors and plough
And also frendes ynough—
4   Thurgh the vertu of my purs.

When my purs gynneth to slake,
And ther is nought in my pak,
They wol seyn, "Go! Farewel, Jakke,
8   Thou shalt namore drynke wyth us."

Thus is al my good i-lorn,
And my purs is al to-torn;
I may pleye me wyth an horn
12   In the stede al of my purs.

Farewel, hors, and farewel, cow,
Farewel, carte, and farewel, plough;
As I pleyde me wyth a bowe
16   I seyde, "God, what is al this?"

Index 3959. MS. Sloane 2593. (*EEC* No. 390.)
Unique text. *c.* 1430.

Gramercy literally, great thanks; thank you
10. **to-torn** torn to pieces; *is* not in MS.

59

God be wyth Trouthe wher he be;
I wolde he were in this contree!

A man that sholde of Trouthe telle,
Wyth grete lordes he may not dwelle;
In trewe storie, as clerkes telle,
4   Trouthe is put in lowe degree.

In ladies chambres cometh he not,
Ther dar Trouthe sette non foot;
Thogh he wolde he may not
8   Come among the heighe meynee.

Wyth men of lawe he hath non space,
They loven Trouthe in non place;
Me thinketh they han a rewely grace
12   That Trouthe is put at swich degree.

In Holy Chirche he may not sitte,
From man to man they shullen him flitte;
It reweth me sore in my wyt—
16   Of Trouthe I have greet pitee.

Index 72. MS. Sloane 2593. (*EEC* No. 385.)
Unique text. *c.* 1430.

8. **heighe meynee** fine company
11. **rewely** rueful, pitiable
14. **flitte** shift, pass on

Religious, that sholden be gode,
If Trouthe come ther, I holde him wood;
They sholden him rende cote and hood
20   And maken him bare for-to flee.

A man that sholde of Trouthe espye,
He moot sechen esily
In the bosom of Mary,
24   For ther he is for sothe.

17. **Religious** those in religious orders
22. **esily** calmly, quietly

60

I passed thurgh a gardyn grene,
I fond an herber made ful newe;
A seemlier sight I have not seen—
4   On ilke tree song a turtel trewe.
Ther-inne a mayden bright of hewe,
And evere she song and nevere she cessed;
Thise were the notes that she gan shewe:
8   *"Verbum caro factum est."*

I axed that mayden what she mente,
She bad me bide and I sholde here;
What she seyde I took good tente—
12   In hir song hadde she vois ful clere.
She seyde, "A prince wythouten pere
Is born and leyd bitwene two beste;
Ther-fore I synge as thou mayst here,
16   *'Verbum caro factum est.'"*

And thurghout that frith as I gan wende,
A blisful song yet herde I mo;
And that was of three shepherdes hende:
20   *"Gloria in excelsis deo."*
I wolde not they hadde faren me fro,
And after hem ful faste I prest;
Than tolde they me that they songen so,
24   For *verbum caro factum est.*

Index 378. Advocates MS. 19. 3. 1. (*RL XV* No. 78.)
Another version in MS. Sloane 2593. *c.* 1430.

8. **Verbum caro factum est** the word is made flesh
14. **beste** = *bestes* beasts
17. **frith** woodland, forest
18. *song* supplied from Sloane MS.

They seyde that song was this to seye:
"To God above be joye and blisse,
For pees in erthe also we preye
28   To alle men that in goodnesse is.
The may that is wythouten mys
Hath born a child bitwene two beste;
She is the cause ther-of, y-wis,
32   That *verbum caro factum est.*

I fared me furthe in that frith,
I mette three comly kynges wyth croune;
I spedde me forth to spekc hem wyth,
36   And on my knees I knelede doun.
The royalest of hem to me gan roune
And seyde, "We fared wel at the feste;
From Bethleem now are we boun,
40   For *verbum caro factum est.*

"For we sawen God bicomen in mannes flessh,
That boot has broght of al oure bale,
Awey oure synnes for-to wasshe;
44   A may him herberd in hir halle,
She socoured him soothly in hir sall
And held that hende in hir arest;
Ful trewely may she telle that tale
48   That *verbum caro factum est.*"

29. **mys** fault
33. **furthe** onward
37. **roune** address
39. **boun** preparing to go
42. **boot** redress, salvation
45. **sall** hall, chamber
46. **arest** abiding-place, chamber

Unto that princesse wol we preye,
As she is bothe moder and mayde;
She be oure help as she wel may
52 To him that in hir lappe was leyd;
To serve him we ben prest and payed,
And ther-to make we oure biheste;
For I herde when she song and seyde,
56 "*Verbum caro factum est.*"

53. **prest and payed** ready and content

61

Go, litel bille, and do me recomaunde
Unto my lady wyth goodly countenaunce;
For trusty messager I thee sende.
4   Preye hire that she make purveiaunce,
For my love, thurgh hir suffraunce,
In hir bosom desireth to reste,
Sith of alle wommen I love hire beste.

8   She is lilye of redolence
Which only may don me plesure;
She is the rose of confidence
Most confortyng to my nature.
12   Unto that lady I me assure,
I wyl hire love and nevere mo:—
Go, litel bille, and sey hire so.

She resteth in my remembraunce
16   Day other nyght wher-so I be;
It is my special daliaunce
For-to remembre hir beautee.
She is enprented in ech degree
20   Wyth yiftes of nature inexplicable,
And eke of grace incomparable.

Index 927. MS. Douce 326 [= Bodl. 21900]. (*RL XV* No. 46.)
Unique text. Fifteenth century.

4. **purveiaunce** provision
5. **suffraunce** permission, allowance
15. *resteth* replaces MS. *restyd*
17. **daliaunce** delight

The cause ther-fore, if she wyl wite,
Why I presume on swich a flour?
24 Sey of hire (for it is i-write)
She is the fairest paramour,
And to man in ech langour
Most soverayn mediatrice:
28 Ther-fore I love that flour of pris.

Hir beautee hoolly to descrive,
Who is he that may suffise?
For sothe no clerk that is alyve,
32 Sith she is only wythouten vice.
Her flavour excedeth the flour-de-lys;
Aforn alle floures I have hire chose
Entierly in myn herte to close.

36 Hire I biseche (sith I not feyne,
But only putte me in hir grace)
That of me she not desdeyne,
Takyng regard at old trespas,—
40 Sith myn entente in every place
Shal be to don hir obeisaunce
And hire to love sauns variaunce.

23. *Why* replaces MS. *Wyll*
27. **mediatrice** mediator, intercessor
30. *he* replaces MS. *she*
41. **obeisaunce** (act of) submission, homage, obeisance

62

    How come alle ye that ben i-broght
    In bondes, ful of bitter bisynesse
    Of erthly lust abidyng in youre thoght?
4 Heer is the reste of al youre bisynesse:
    Heer is the port of pees, and restfulnesse
    To hem that stonde in stormes of disese,
    Only refuge to wrecches in distresse,
8 And al comfort of myschief and mysese.

Index 1254. Royal MS. 9. C. ii. (*RL XV* No. 164.)
This is Meter 10, Book III, of John Walton's translation (1410) of
    Boethius's *De Consolatione Philosophiae*; multiple copies. Early
    fifteenth century.

63

I moot go walke the wode so wilde,
　And wandren heer and ther
　In drede and deedly fere;
4　For wher I trusted I am begiled,
　And al for oon.

Thus am I banysshed from my blisse
　By craft and fals pretence,
8　Fautles wythoute offence;
　As of retourn no certeyn is,
　And al for fere of oon.

My bed shal be under the grene-wode tree,
12　A toft of brakes under myn hed,
　As oon from joye were fled;
　Thus from my lyf day by day I flee,
　And al for oon.

16　The rennyng stremes shullen be my drynke,
　Accornes shullen be my fode;
　No-thyng may do me good
　But whan of thy beautee I do thenke—
20　And al for love of oon.

Index 1333. Huntington MS. EL 1160. (*SL XIV-XV* No. 20.)
One other text and fragment. Fifteenth century.

9. **certeyn** certainty
12. **toft of brakes** tuft of ferns or bracken

64

Go, litel ryng, to that ilke swete
That hath myn herte in hir demeyne,
And loke thou knele doun at hir feet
4   Bisechyng hire she wolde not desdeyne
On hir smale fyngres thee to streyne;
Than I wyl thee seye boldely:
"My maister wolde that he were I."

Index 932. Royal MS. 17. D. vi. (*SL XIV-XV* No. 95.)
Unique text. Fifteenth century.

2. **demeyne** possession, demesne
5. **streyne** encircle, clasp

65

Fressh lusty beautee joyned wyth gentilesse,
   Demure, apert, glad chere wyth governaunce,
Ech thyng demened by avysenesse,
4   Prudent of speche, wysdom of daliaunce,
   Gentilesse wyth wommanly plesaunce,
     Hevenly eyen, aungelik of visage—
     Al this hath nature set in thyn ymage.

8 Wyfly trouthe wyth Penelope,
   And wyth Grisilde parfit pacience,
Like Polixene fairely on-to see,
   Of bountee beautee having the excellence
12   Of Quene Alceste, and al the diligence
   Of faire Dido, princesse of Cartage—
    Al this hath nature set in thyn ymage.

Index 869. Trinity Coll. Camb. MS. 600. (*SL XIV-XV* No. 131.)
By John Lydgate (?1370-1449). One other text.

2. **Demure, apert** reserved, frank, open; **governaunce** government, self-control
3. **avysenesse** deliberation
4. **daliaunce** conversation
8. **Wyfly** womanly; **Penelope** Odysseus' wife ingeniously withstood suitors who thought her husband was dead. See Homer's *Odyssey*.
9. **Grisilde** In legend, her perfect patience in suffering outrageous cruelty is ultimately rewarded. See Chaucer's *Clerk's Tale*.
10. **Polixene** Daughter of Priam, king of Troy; she was sacrificed at the end of the Trojan War.
11. **bountee** excellence, virtue
12. **Alceste** The only one willing to die in place of her husband Admetus, Alcestis was rescued by Heracles.
13. **Dido** Having fallen in love with Aeneas, Dido killed herself when he left her. Cf. Chaucer's *Legend of Good Women*.

Of Niobe the seur perseveraunce,
16   Of Adriane the grete stedefastnesse,
Assured trouthe, void of variaunce;
     Wyth yong Tesbee ensaumple of kyndenesse,
     Of Cleopatres abidyng stablenesse,
20   Mekenesse of Hester void of al outrage—
     Al this hath nature set in thyn ymage.

Beautee surmountyng wyth faire Rosemounde,
     And wyth Isoude for-to ben secree,
24 And like Judith in vertue to habounde,
     And seemlynesse wyth Quene Bersabee,
     Innocence, freedom, and heighe bountee,
     Fulfilled of vertue void of al damage—
28   Al this hath nature set in thyne ymage.

---

15. **Niobe** Punished for pride by the gods, the grieving Niobe was turned to stone.
16. **Adriane** Ariadne was abandoned on an island by her husband Theseus. Cf. Chaucer's *Legend of Good Women.*
18. **Tesbee** Thisbe, lover of Pyramus. Cf. Chaucer's *Legend of Good Women.*
19. **Cleopatra** Cf. Chaucer's *Legend of Good Women* and Plutarch's account of Antony in *Lives of the Noble Grecians and Romans.*
20. **Hester** Esther. See the Book of Esther. **outrage** intemperance
22. **Rosemounde** Rosamond "The Fair," mistress of Henry II of England.
23. **Isoude** Isolt (Iseult), in the Tristan legends; **secree** trusty, secret
24. **Judith** Slayer of Holofernes. See the apocryphal Book of Judith.
25. **Bersabee** Bathsheba. See II Samuel.

What sholde I more reherce of wommanhede?
　　Thou best the mirour and verray exemplaire
Of whom that word and thoght accorde in dede;
32　　And in my sight fairest of alle faire,
　　Humble and meke, benigne and debonaire,
　　　Of othere vertues wyth al the surplusage
　　　Which that nature hath set in thyn ymage.

36　I see non lak but only that Daunger
　　　Hath in thee voided Mercy and Pitee,
That thee list not wyth thyn excellence
　　Upon thy servauntes goodly for-to see;
40　　Wher-on ful sore I compleyne me
　　　That Routhe is void to my disavauntage,
　　　Sith alle thise vertues ben set in thyn ymage.

　　　　　　L'envoye
　　Go, litel balade, and recomaund me
44　　Unto hir pitee, hir mercy, and hir grace—
But firste be war aforn that thou wel see
　　Desdayn and Daunger ben void out of that place;
　　For elles thou mayst have leiser non nor space
48　　Trewely to hire to don my message,
　　　Which hath alle vertues set in hir ymage.

30. **exemplaire** perfect specimen
34. **surplusage** surplus, abundance
41. **Routhe** Pity, Compassion
45. **see** = *seest*
47. **leiser . . . space** opportunity . . . occasion

66

So faire, so fressh, so goodly on-to see,
   So wel demened in al youre governaunce
   That to myn herte it is a greet plesaunce
4 Of youre goodnesse whan I remembre me;
   And truste fully wher that evere I be
   I wyl abide under youre obeisaunce,—
So faire, so fressh, so goodly on-to see,
8   So wel demened in al youre governaunce.
For in my thoght ther is no mo but ye
   Whom I have served wythoute repentaunce:
   Wher-fore, I preye you, sethe to my grevaunce,
12 And put aside al myn adversitee,—
So faire, so fressh, so goodly on-to see,
   So wel demened in al youre governaunce.

Index 3162. Paris Bibl. nat. MS. f. fr. 25458. (*SL XIV-XV* No. 182.)
By Charles d'Orleans (1391–1455). One other text.

2. **governaunce** goverment, self-control, demeanor (In this, as well as
the other poems by Charles d'Orleans (Nos. 67 and 71), the pronoun of
address, i.e., second person, is plural in form, for politeness, even though
the referent may be singular.)
6. **obeisaunce** obedience, (act of) attention, homage
11. **sethe** look (to), or = *see thou?*

67

Go forth, myn herte, wyth my lady;
   Loke that ye spare no bisynesse
   To serve hire wyth swich lowlynesse
4 That ye gete hir grace and mercy;
   Preye hire ofte-tymes prively
   That she kepe trewely hir promesse:
Go forth, myn herte, wyth my lady,
8   Loke that ye spare no bisynesse.
I moot as a herteles body
   Abide allone in hevynesse,
   And ye shal dwelle wyth youre maistresse
12 In plesaunce glad and myrie,—
Go forth, myn herte, wyth my lady,
   Loke that ye spare no bisynesse.

Index 922. Paris Bibl. nat. f. fr. 25458. (*SL XIV-XV* No. 183.)
By Charles d'Orleans (1391–1455). Two other texts.

 2. **bisynesse** diligence, careful attention
10. **hevynesse** dejection, sorrow

68

Go herte, hurt wyth adversitee,
    And lat my lady thy woundes see;
    And sey hire this, as I seye thee:
4   Farewel my joye, and welcome peyne,
    Til I see my lady ageyn.

Index 925. MS. Ashmole 191 IV [= Bodl. 6668]. (*SL XIV-XV* No. 155.)
With music (a madrigal). Unique text. *c.* 1445.

69

Allas, departyng is ground of wo,—
    Other song can I not synge.
    But why parte I my lady fro,
4   Sith love was cause of oure metyng?
    The bittre teres of hir wepyng
        Myn herte hath perced so mortally,
    That to the deeth it wil be brynge
8   But if I see hire hastily.

Index 146. MS. Ashmole 191 [= Bodl. 6668]. (*SL XIV-XV* No. 156.)
With music. Unique text. *c.* 1445.

Now wolde I fayn som myrthes make
Al only for my ladies sake,
   Whan I hire see;
4 But now I am so fer fro hire
   It wol not be.

Thogh I be fer out of hir sight,
I am hir man bothe day and nyght,
8   And so wol be:
Ther-fore wolde as I love hire
   She lovede me.

Whan she is myrie than am I glad,
12 Whan she is sory than am I sad,
   And cause is why:—
For he lyveth not that loveth hire
   So wel as I.

16 She seyth that she hath seen it writen
That 'selden seen is soon forgeten.'
   It is not so,
For, in good feith, save only hire
20   I love no mo.

Wher-fore I preye bothe nyght and day
That she may caste al care awey
   And lyve in reste,
24 And evermore wher-evere she be
   To love me best;

Index 2381. MS. Ashmole 191 [= Bodl. 6668]. (*SL XIV-XV* No. 171.) Another text in Camb. Univ. MS. Ff. 1. 6. *c.* 1445.

And I to hire to be so trewe,
And nevere to chaunge for no newe,
28   Unto myn ende,
And that I may in hir servise
Evere to amende.

71

My gostly fader, I me confesse,
    First to God and than to you,
    That at a wyndow (wost thou how?)
4 I stal a cosse of greet sweetnesse,
Which don was out avysenesse;
    But it is don, not undon, now,
My gostly fader, I me confesse,
8   First to God and than to you.
But I restore it shal douteles
    Ageyn, if so be that I mowe,—
    And that to God I make avow,
12 And elles I axe foryifnesse.
My gostly fader, I me confesse
First to God and than to you.

Index 2243. Harley MS. 682. (*SL XIV-XV* No. 185.)
By Charles d'Orleans (1391–1455). Unique text.

2. **you** = *thee*
5. **avysenesse** deliberation
10. **mowe** for *mote* (subjunctive), or *may*
11. **avow** a solemn promise, oath; MS. reads: *And that god y make a vow*

As in thee resteth my joye and confort,
  Thy disese is my mortal peyne;
Soon God sende me swich report
4   That may conforte myn herte in every veyne.
  Who but thou may me susteyne,
    Or of my greef be the remedye,
    But thou soon have amendement of thy maladye,

8 Which is to me the hevyest remembraunce
  That evere can be thoght in any creature;
Myn herte hangyng thus in balaunce
  Til I have knoweleche and verraily sure
12 That God in thee hath list don this cure,
    Of thy disese to have allegeaunce
    And to be releved of al thy grevaunce.

Index 383. Camb. Univ. MS. Ff. 1. 6. (*SL XIV-XV* No. 164.)
Unique text. Before 1500.

13. **allegeaunce** alleviation, relief

Allas, allas the while!
Thoghte I on no gile,
  So have I good chaunce.
Allas, allas the while—
  That evere I coude daunce!

Ledde I the daunce a mydsomer day;
I made smal trippes, soth for-to seye.
Jak, oure holy water clerke, cam by the weye,
4 And he loked me upon, he thoghte that I was gay.
   Thoghte I on no gile.

Jak, oure holy water clerk, the yonge strippelyng,
For the chesoun of me he cam to the ryng;
8 And he tripped on my too and made a twynkelyng—
Evere he cam neer, he spared for no thyng.
   Thoghte I on no gile.

Jak, I wot, pryed in my faire face;
12 He thoghte me ful worly, so have I good grace.
As we turnden oure daunce in a narwe place,
Jak bad me the mouth—a kissing ther was.
   Thoghte I on no gile.

Index 1849. Caius Coll. Camb. MS. 383. (*SL XIV-XV* No. 28.)
Unique text. Expansions and emendation as in *SL XIV-XV* No. 28. *c.*
   1450.

2. **trippes** steps in dancing
6. **strippelyng** a youth just passed into manhood, stripling
7. **For the chesoun of me** because of me
8. **too** toe; **twynkelyng** wink
11. **pryed** looked searchingly
12. **worly** attractive

16   Jak tho bigan to roune in myn ere,
     "Loke that thou be privee and graunte that thou bere;
     A paire white gloves I have to thy were."
     "Gramercy, Jak," that was myn answere.
20   Thoghte I on no gile.

     Soon after evensong Jak me mette:
     "Com hom after thy gloves that I thee bihete."
     Whan I to his chambre cam, doun he me sette;
24   From him myghte I not go whan we were mette.
         Thoghte I on no gile.

     Shetes and chalones, I wot, were i-spred;
     For sothe tho Jak and I wenten to bed.
28   He priked and he praunced—nolde he nevere lynne:
     It was the muriest nyght that evere I cam inne.
         Thoghte I on no gile.

     Whan Jak hadde don tho he rong the belle;
32   Al nyght ther he made me to dwelle.
     Oft, I trewe, we hadden i-served the ragged devil of
             helle;
     Of other smal bourdes kepe I not to telle.
         Thoghte I on no gile.

16. **roune in myn ere** whisper in my ear
18. **were** i.e., wearing
26. **Shetes and chalones** sheets and blankets
28. **nolde** = *ne wolde*; **lynne** cease
33. **trewe** suppose; **ragged** shaggy
34. **bourdes** frivolities, delights

36   The other day at pryme I cam hom, as I wene,
      Mete I may dame copped and kene:
      "Sey, thou strong strompet, wher hastow ben?
      Thy trippyng and thy daunsyng, wel it wol be sene!"
40   Thoghte I on no gile.

      Evere by oon and by oon my dame raughte me clout.
      Evere I bar it privee whil that I moghte,
      Til my girdel aros, my womb wex out:
44   "Yvele i-spun yerne evere it wol out."
          Thoghte I on no gile.

36. **The other day at pryme** the next morning at dawn (before sun-up)
37. **copped and kene** peevish, bad-tempered and harsh
38. **hastow** = *hast thou*
41. **Evere by oon and by oon** again and again; **raughte me clout** dealt
    me a clout, a cuff (with the hand)
42. **moghte** = *myghte*
44. **Yvele i-spun yerne** ill-spun yarn

74

Care awey, awey, awey,
Murnyng awey,
   I am forsake,
   Another is take,
No more murne I may.

I am sory for hir sake,
   I may wel ete and drynke;
Whan I slepe I may not wake,
4   So muche on hire I thenke.

I am broght in swich a bale,
   And broght in swich a pyne,
Whan I rise up of my bed
8   Me liste wel to dyne.

I am broght in swich a pyne
   I-broght in swich a bale,
Whan I have riche gode wyne
12   Me liste drynke non ale.

Index 1280. Caius Coll. Camb. MS. 383. (*SL XIV-XV* No. 37.)
Unique text. *c.* 1450.

I may wel sike for grevous is my peyne
Now to departe from thee this sodeynly;
My faire swete herte, thou causest me to compleyne;
4   For lak of thee I stonde ful pitously
Al in disconfort, wythouten remedye.
Most in my mynde, my lady soverayne,
Allas, for wo! departyng hath me slayn.

8   Farewel, my myrthe, and chief of my confort;
My joye is turned into hevynesse
Til I ageyn to thee may resorte;
As for the tyme I am but recureles,
12   Like to a figure which that is herteles.
Wyth thee it is, God wot, I may not feyne,
Allas, for wo! departyng hath me slayn.

Yet not wythstondyng, for al my grevaunce,
16   It shal be taken right paciently,
And thenk it is to me but a plesaunce
For thee to suffre a greet deel more trewely;
Wyl nevere chaunge but kepe unfeynyngly
20   Wyth al my myght to be bothe trewe and playn:
Allas, for wo! departyng hath me slayn.

Index 1331. Camb. Univ. MS. Ff. 1. 6. (*SL XIV-XV* No. 169.)
Unique text. *c.* 1470.

11. **recureles** lacking (in means or hope) of recovery

Faire, fresshest erthly creature
That evere the sonne over-shon,
The best and the shapliest figure
4   That kynde hath wroght of blood and bon—

.   .   .   .

Whos I have ben, am, and evere shal be in oon:
Wyth al my poure hertes lowe servise
8   I me recomaunde on every humble wyse
That tonge can telle or herte devise,
To thee that alle my lyves are on.

My trouthe to thee I write
12   As he that is wyth wo oppressed sore,
Compleynyng, as I dar endite,
My hele that is evermore.
Al-thogh thise wordes rude ben and lite,
16   Be thou not greved wyth me there-fore.
Biseche I thy noble grace,
And hold not thy debonaire face
Defouled to see this whan thou hast space,
20   That boot is of my sorwe sore.

Index 754. MS. Douce 95 [= Bodl. 21669]. (*SL XIV-XV* No. 199.)
(Among the difficulties in this text are the apparent omission of a line
    after line 4 and the corruption of line 36.) Unique text.
Fifteenth century.

5. *and*, replacing MS. *had*
12. *As he*, replacing MS. *as she*
16. *Be thou*, replacing MS. *ye be*
19. *thou hast*, replacing MS. *y haue*, probably for *ye haue*
20. **boot** cure

Thy goodnesse also I biseche
    Consider al myn hertes care;
Thou lette thy mercy over me strecche,
24   And that causeth my mysfare
(As this lettre shal thee shewe),
    My lyves ende, my blisse bare.
      Thou vouchesauf to me to dele
28   Right as thee list, siknesse or hele,
      Lyf or deeth, wo or wele —
Al in thy grace I put my fare.

The fresshe beautee of thy comlyhede
32   So hote sette myn herte on fyr,
Whan I saw first thy maydenhede,
    That evere sith swich desire
Have I had to serve thee
36   Whil I may tire;
      That evere sith wyth cold of hete,
      Wyth hete of cold myn herte is bete,
      I nam but deed but thou me hete
40   Thy love ageyn to quite my hire.

From which thou mayst me releve,
    Wolde thou vouchesauf to do so,
And from alle sores myn herte reve,
44   Wyth a goodly word or two;

30. *I* not in MS.
31. **comlyhede** beauty, fairness
39. **hete** promise, assure
40. **quite my hire** repay (me for) my service
43. **reve** take away, separate

Myghte I fele in word or other
That thou wast not my fo.
In world a wight a thousand dele
48 Was nevere sonner broght to hele,
For and thou lovede me trewely lele
Wolde I nevere have joyes mo.

Fairest of faire, this lettre lite,
52 That chief is of my peynes smerte
(Al can I not wel endite),—
Lat thise wordes synke in thyn herte.
For al my wele and wo, y-wis,
56 Thus I conclude in wordes shorte;
But if thou rewe upon my peyne
And bryne my bale to blisse ageyn,
Certes I can not elles seyn
60 But deeth I may not a-sterte.

48. **sonner** sooner
49. **lele** loyally, faithfully
57. *rewe* for MS. *rued*
60. **a-sterte** escape

77

Farewel, this world! I take my leve for evere,—
I am arested to appere at Goddes face.
O myghtyful God, thou knowest that I hadde levere
4 Thanne al this world to have oon houre space
To make asseth for al my grete trespas.
Myn herte, allas, is broken for that sorwe!
Som ben this day that shullen not ben to-morwe.

8 This lyf, I see, is but a chery-feire,—
Alle thynges passen and so moot I algate.
To-day I sat ful royal in a chaire
Til subtil Deeth knokked at my yate
12 And unavysed he seyde to me, "Chekmat!"
Lo! how subtil he maketh a divors,
And wormes to fede he hath heer leyd my cors.

Speketh softe, ye folk, for I am leyd a-sleep,—
16 I have my dreem, in trust is muche tresoun.
From Dethes hold fayne wolde I make a leep,
But my wysdom is turned into feble resoun.
I see this worldes joye lasteth but a sesoun:

Index 769. Trin. Coll. Camb. MS. 1157, with readings from Balliol
Coll. Oxf. MS. 354. (*RL XV* No. 149.)
Fifteenth century.

3. **I hadde levere** I would rather, I would more willingly
5. **asseth** amends, expiation
8. **lyf . . . is but a chery-feire** life is transitory
9. **algate** in any case, at any rate
11. **yate** gate
14. **cors** corpse
17. **hold** stronghold; captivity

20　Wolde to God I hadde remembred me biforn!
　　I seye namore but beth war of an horn.

　　This feble world, so fals and so unstable,
　　Promoteth his lovers for a litel while;
24　But atte laste he yeveth hem a bable,
　　Whan his peynted trouthe is turned into gile.
　　Experience causeth me the trouthe to compile,
　　Thenkyng this, to late, allas! that I bigan,
28　For folye and hope disceiven many a man.

　　Farewel, my frendes! The tide abideth no man,—
　　I moot departe hennes, and so shullen ye;
　　But in this passage the beste song that I can
32　Is *Requiem Eternum*—I preye God graunte it me.
　　Whan I have ended al myn adversitee,
　　Graunte me in paradys to have a mansioun,
　　That shedde his blood for my redempcioun.

21. **horn** i.e., the summons to Judgment
24. **bable** bauble, plaything
25. **peynted** pretended, disguised

134

78

In what estat so evere I be,
Timor mortis conturbat me.

As I went in a myrie morwenynge
I herde a brid bothe wepe and synge;
This was the tenour of hir talkynge—
4 *Timor mortis conturbat me.*

I axed that brid what she mente.
"I am a musket bothe faire and gent;
For drede of deeth I am al shent:
8 *Timor mortis conturbat me.*

"Whan I shal deye I knowe no day,
What contree or place I can not seye;
Wher-fore this song synge I may—
12 *Timor mortis conturbat me.*

"Jhesu Crist, whan he sholde deye,
To his Fader he gan seye,
'Fader,' he seyde, 'in trinitee,
16 *Timor mortis conturbat me.'*

Index 375. MS. Eng. poet. e. I [= Bodl. 29734]. (*EEC* No. 370.)
One other partial text. *c.* 1470.

estat circumstance, condition, estate
Timor mortis conturbat me Fear of death distresses me
3. **tenour** substance, purport
6. **musket** (male) sparrowhawk
7. **shent** rendered useless, brought to ruin

"Alle cristen peple biholde and see
This world is but a vanytee,
And repleet wyth necessitee.
20 *Timor mortis conturbat me.*

"Wake I or slepe, ete or drynke,
Whan I on my laste ende do thenke,
For greet fere my soule doth shrynke:
24 *Timor mortis conturbat me.*"

God graunte us grace Him for-to serve,
And be at oure ende whan we sterve,
And from the feend He us preserve!
28 *Timor mortis conturbat me.*

23. **fere** fear
26. **sterve** die

79

Evermore, wher-so-evere I be,
The drede of deeth doth trouble me.

As I went me for-to solace
I herde a man sike and seye, "Allas,
Of me now thus stondeth the cas:
4   The drede of deeth doth trouble me.

"I have ben lord of tour and toun;
I sette noght by my grete renoun,
For deeth wol plukke it al adoun:
8   The drede of deeth doth trouble me.

"Whan I shal deye I am not seur,
In what contree or in what houre;
Wher-fore I sobbyng seye to my power,
12   'The drede of deeth doth trouble me.'

"Whan my soule and my body departed shullen be,
Of my juggement no man can telle me,
Nor of my place wher that I shal be:
16   Ther-fore drede of deeth doth trouble me.

"Jhesu Crist, whan that he sholde suffre his passioun,
To his Fader he seyde wyth greet devocioun,
'This is the cause of my intercessioun:
20   The drede of deeth doth trouble me.'

Index 376. MS. Eng. poet. e. I [= Bodl. 29734]. (*EEC* No. 371.)
Unique text. *c.* 1470.

1. **me . . . solace** delight, amuse myself
7. *adoun* for MS. *downe*
13. **departed** divided, separated

"Alle cristen peple, beth ye wyse and ware,—
This world is but a chery-feire,
Repleet wyth sorwe and fulfilled wyth care:
24   Ther-fore the drede of deeth doth trouble me.

"Whether that I be myrie or good wyne drynke,
Whan that I do on my laste day thenke,
It maketh my soule and body to shrynke,
28   For the drede of deeth sore troubleth me."

Jhesu us graunte Him so to honoure
That at oure ende He may be oure socour
And kepe us from the fendes power,
32   For than drede of deeth shal not trouble me.

22. **This world is but a chery-feire** i.e., the world (and its pleasures) are
    transient

80

Care awey, awey, awey,
Care awey for evermore!

Al that I may swynke or swete,
My wyf it wyl bothe drynke and ete;
If I seye aught she wyl me bete—
4 Care-ful is myn herte ther-for!

If I seye aught of hire but good,
She loketh on me as she were wood,
And wyl me cloute aboute the hood—
8 Care-ful is myn herte ther-for!

If she wyl to the gode ale ride,
Me moste trotte al by hir side;
And whan she drynketh I moot abide—
12 Care-ful is myn herte ther-for!

If I seye, "It shal be thus,"
She seyth, "Thou lyest, cherl, y-wus!
Wenestow to overcome me thus?"
16 Care-ful is myn herte ther-for!

Index 210. MS. Eng. poet. e. I [= Bodl. 29734]. (*SL XIV-XV* No. 44.)
Unique text. *c.* 1470.

1. **swynke** labor
3. *If* for MS. &
7. **me moste** I must
14. **y-wus** = *y-wis*
15. **wenestow** = *wenest thou* do you imagine (expect)

If any man have swich a wyfe to lede,
He shal knowe how *iudicare* cam in the crede;
Of his penaunce God do him mede!
20   Care-ful is myn herte ther-for!

17. **lede** deal with
18. **how iudicare cam in the crede** "The meaning here seems to be that the husband is undergoing a 'hell on earth,' and that this punishment should be credited to him!" (*SL XIV-XV*, p. 240)

140

A, a, a, a,
Yet I love wher-so I go.

In al this world nis a murier lyf
Thanne is a yong man wythouten a wyf,
For he may lyven wythouten strif
4   In every place wher-so he go.

In every place he is loved over alle
Among maydens grete and smale—
In daunsyng, in pipyng, and rennyng at the balle,
8   In every place wher-so he go.

They leten lighte by housebonde-men
Whan they at the balle renne;
They casten her love to yonge men
12   In every place wher-so he go.

Than seyn maydens, "Farewel, Jakke,
Thy love is pressed al in thy pak;
Thou berest thy love bihynde thy bak,
16   In every place wher-so thou go."

Index 1468. MS. Eng. poet. e. I [= Bodl. 29734]. (*SL XIV-XV* No. 8.)
Unique text. *c.* 1470.

7. **rennyng at the balle** stool ball, probably, "played by men and women, a simple game resembling cricket" (*SL XIV-XV*, p. 230)
9. **leten lighte by** think little of

Bryng us in good ale, and bryng us in good ale!
Fou oure blessed Ladies sake, bryng us in good ale!

Bryng us in no broun breed, for that is made of bren,
Nor bryng us in no white breed, for ther-inne is
    no game—
  But bryng us in good ale.

4 Bryng us in no beef, for there is many bones,
But bryng us in good ale, for that goth doun at ones—
  And bryng us in good ale.

Bryng us in no bacoun, for that is passyng fat,
8 But bryng us in good ale, and yif us ynough of that—
  And bryng us in good ale.

Bryng us in no moton, for that is ofte lene,
Nor bryng us in to trypes, for they ben selden clene—
12   But bryng us in good ale.

Bryng us in no eyren, for ther are many shelles,
But bryng us in good ale, and yif us no thyng elles—
  And bryng us in good ale.

16 Bryng us in to butter, for ther-inne are many heres,
Nor bryng us in no pigges flessh, for that wyl make us
    bores—
  But bryng us in good ale.

Index 549. MS. Eng. poet. e. I [= Bodl. 29734]. (*SL XIV-XV* No. 13.)
One other (shorter) text. *c.* 1470.

13. **eyren** eggs

Bryng us in no podynges, for ther-inne is al gotes blood,
20   Nor bryng us in no venysoun, for that is not for
        oure good—
    But bryng us in good ale.

Bryng us in no capons flessh, for that is ofte dere,
Nor bryng us in no dokes flessh, for they slobere in
        the mere,
24   But bryng us in good ale.

---

19. *gotes blood* for MS. *Godes good*
20. *oure good* for MS. *owr blod*
22. **dere** costly, expensive

83

Nowel, el, el, el, el!
I thonke it a mayden everydel.

The firste day whan Crist was born,
Ther sprong a rose out of a thorn
To save mankynde that was forlorn:
4   I thonke it a mayden everydel.

In an oxe-stall that child was founde;
In poure clothyng the child was wounde;
He suffred many a deedly wounde:
8   I thonke it a mayden everydel.

A gerlond of thornes on his hed was set,
A shape spere to his herte was smyt;
The Jewes seyden, "Tak thou that!"
12   I thonke it a mayden everydel.

The Jewes dide crien her parlement
On the day of juggement;
They weren aferd they sholde ben shent:
16   I thonke it a mayden everydel.

Index 3344. MS. Eng. poet. e. I [= Bodl. 29734]. (*EEC* No. 41.)
Unique text. *c.* 1470.

13. **dide crien** gave public, oral announcement (for the purpose of summoning)
15. **shent** ruined, brought to nothing; *ben* replaces MS. *hem*

144

To the piler he was bounde,
To his herte a spere was stongen;
For us he suffred a deedly wounde:
20   I thonke it a mayden everydel.

---

18. **stongen** (MS. *stunggyn*) provides neither sense nor rhyme; possibly the
line should read: *His herte was stongen to the grounde* (**grounde** base,
bottom)

84

Of a rose, a lovely rose,
Of a rose I synge a song.

Lythe and listneth, bothe olde and yinge,
How the rose bigan to sprynge;
A fairer rose to oure likyng
4   Sprong ther nevere in kynges lond.

Five braunches of that rose ther ben,
The which ben bothe faire and shene;
Of a mayden, Mary, hevene quene,
8   Out of hir bosom the braunche sprong.

The firste braunche was of greet honour,
That blessed Mary sholde bere the flour;
Ther cam an aungel out hevene tour
12   To breke the develes bond.

The seconde braunche was greet of myghte
That sprong upon Cristemasse nyght;
The sterre shon and lemed bright
16   That man sholde see it bothe day and nyght.

Index 1914. MS. Eng. poet. e. I [= Bodl. 29734]. (*EEC* No. 175A.)
Also in Balliol Coll. Oxf. MS. 354. *c.* 1470.

1. **Lythe** listen (imperative plural); **olde and yinge** i.e., everybody
(**yinge** = *yonge*)
15. **lemed** shone, gleamed

The thridde braunche gan sprynge and sprede;
Three kynges than the braunche gan lede
Tho to Oure Lady in hir child-bed,—
20   Into Bethleem that braunche sprong right.

The ferthe braunche, it sprong to helle
The develes power for-to felle,
That no soule ther-in sholde dwelle,
24   The braunche so blessedfully sprong.

The fifte braunche, it was so swote,
It sprong to hevene bothe crop and rote
In every bale to ben our boot,
28   So blessedly it sprong.

---

18. *the* for MS. *to*
25. **swote** = *swete*
26. **crop and rote** top and root, i.e., entirely

85

Of alle the enemies that I can fynde
The tonge is most enemy to mankynde.

Wyth pitee moved I am constreyned
  To synge a song for youre confort,
How that diverse have compleyned
4   Of tonge untrewe and il report,
  Seying thus wythoute desport:—

This tonge is instrument of discord,
  Causyng werre and greet distaunce
8 Bitwene the subjet and the lord,
  The parfit cause of every grevaunce;
  Wher-fore I synge wythoute displesaunce:—

Thogh that prestes ben nevere so pacient
12   In toun, citee, or in court royal,
Thogh the religious ben nevere so obedient,
  Yet an il tonge wyl trouble hem alle;
  Wher-for this song reherce I shal:—

16 If he that ille by another do seye
  His propre fautes wolde biholde,
How ofte-tymes him-self were out of the wey,
  Silence to him than sholde ben gold,
20   And wyth me to synge he wolde ben bold:—

Index 4198. Bodl. Lib. MS. Eng. poet. e. I [=Bodl. 29734]. (*EEC* No. 342.)

Unique text. *c.* 1470.

7. **distaunce** quarreling
13. **religious** i.c., those in religious orders

From this tonge, a venymous serpent,
   Defend us, Fader, to Thee we preye,
As Thou unto us thy Sone has sent
24   For-to ben born this present day,
   Lest that we synge and evermore seye:

Of alle the enemies that I can fynde
The tonge is most enemy to mankynde.

86

Sodeynly affrayed, half wakyng, half slepyng,
And greetly dismayde, a womman sat wepyng:

Wyth favour in hir face fer passyng my resoun,
And of hir sore wepyng this was the enchesoun:
Hir sone in hir lappe lay, she seyde, slayn by tresoun.
4   If wepyng myghte ripe ben, it semed than in sesoun.
   "Jhesu!" so she sobbed,
   So hir sone was bobbed
   And of his lyf robbed,
8   Seying thise wordes, as I seye thee:
"Who can not wepe, come lerne at me."

I seyde I coude not wepe, I was so hard-herted.
She answerde me wyth wordes shortly that smerted:
12   "Lo, nature shal meve thee, thou most be converted.
Thyn owene fader this nyght is deed," lo, thus she
      thwarted,
   "So my sone is bobbed
   And of his lyf robbed."
16   For sothe than I sobbed,
Verifying the wordes she seyde to me:
Who can not wepe may lerne at thee.

Index 4189. John Rylands Library, Manchester. Lat. MS. 395. (*RL XV* No. 9.)

One other text. Fifteenth century.

2. **enchesoun** reason, occasion
6. **bobbed** buffeted (and mocked)
12. **meve** move
13. **thwarted** retorted

"Now breek, herte, I thee preye! This cors lieth so rewely,
20 So beten, so wounded, entreted so Jewely,
What wight may me biholde and wepe not? Non, trewely,
To see my dede dere sone lie bledyng, lo, this newely."
    Ay stille she sobbed
24   So hir sone was bobbed
    And of his lyf robbed,
Newyng the wordes, as I seye thee:
"Who can not wepe, come lerne at me."

28 On me she caste hir eye, seyde, "See, man, thy brother!"
She kiste him and seyde, "Swete, am I not thy moder?"
In swownyng she fil ther, it wolde ben non other.
I not which more deedly, that oon or that other.
32   Yet she revived and sobbed
    So hir sone was bobbed
    And of his lyf robbed.
"Who can not wepe"—this was the laye—
36 And wyth that word she vanisht awey.

19. **rewely** ruefully, pitably
20. **entreted** treated, dealt with; **Jewely** like a Jew
30. *swownyng* for MS. *sownyng*
31. **not** = *ne wot* know not
35. **laye** strain, purport

I wende to deeth, knight stith in stour,
Thurgh fight in feeld I wan the flour;
No fightes me taughte the deeth to quelle—
4   I wende to deeth, sooth I you telle.

I wende to deeth, a kyng, y-wis;
What helpeth honour or worldes blisse?
Deeth is to man the kynde way—
8   I wende to be cladde in cley.

I wende to deeth, clerk ful of skile,
That coude wyth word men marre and dile;
Soon has me made the deeth an ende—
12   Beth war wyth me! to deeth I wende.

Index 1387. Cotton MS. Faustina B.vii, Part II. (*RL XV* No. 158A.)
Two other texts. Fifteenth century.

1. **stith in stour** stout in battle
4. First *I* not in MS.
9. **clerk** one in religious orders
10. **marre and dile** bewilder and assuage; ruin and conceal

Al worldly welthe passed me fro;
Nunc in pulvere dormio.

I hadde richesse, I hadde my helthe,
I hadde honour and worldly welthe;
Yet decth hath take me hennes by stelthe.
4   *Nunc in pulvere dormio.*

Of al solas I hadde my wylle,
Of mete and drynke having my fille;
Yet deeth hath smyt me wyth his bille.
8   *Nunc in pulvere dormio.*

I hadde beautee in hond and face,
I hadde confort in every cas;
Yet, arested wyth dethes mace,
12   *Nunc in pulvere dormio.*

I hadde musik, I hadde swete song,
And other game and myrthe among;
Yet deeth hath felled me wyth his prong.
16   *Nunc in pulvere dormio.*

I hadde connyng, wysdom, and wyt;
Manhod and strengthe in me were knit;
Yet deeth hath broght me to my pit.
20   *Nunc in pulvere dormio.*

Index 1298. Camb. Univ. MS. Ee. 1. 12. (*EEC* No. 353.)
Unique text. By James Ryman. *c.* 1490.

Nunc in pulvere dormio Now I sleep in dust
5. **solas** amusement, pleasure
7. **bill** instrument for pruning or cutting; sword, ax
19. **pit** grave

O man, which art erthe by thy kynde,
Whos lyf is but a blast of wynd,
This dredeful word bere in thy mynde:
24   *"Nunc in pulvere dormio."*

Whil thou art heer, man, wel thee gide,
For thou shalt not ay heer abide;
But thou shalt seye, man, at a tide:
28   *"Nunc in pulvere dormio."*

Almyghty God, graunte us alle grace
Wel to expende oure tyme and space
Er-that we come unto that cas.
32   *Nunc in pulvere dormio.*

89

Mary hath born allone
The Sone of God in trone.

That mayden mylde hir childe dide kepe
　　As modres don echoon,
But hir dere Sone ful sore dide wepe
4　　For synful man allone.

She rokked Him and song "Lullay,"
　　But evere He made greet mone;
"Dere sone," she seyde, "tel, I thee preye,
8　　Why Thou dost wepe allone."

"Moder," He seyde, "I shal be slayn,
　　That synne dide nevere non,
And suffre deeth wyth woful peyne,—
12　　Ther-fore I wepe allone."

"Lullay," she seyde, "sleep and be stille,
　　And lat be al thy mone;
For al thyng is at thyn owene wylle
16　　In hevene and erthe allone."

"Moder," He seyde, "how sholde I slepe?
　　How sholde I leve my mone?
I have more cause to sobbe and wepe
20　　Sith I shal deye allone."

Index 3284. Camb. Univ. MS. Ee. 1. 12. (*EEC* No. 154.)
Unique text. By James Ryman. *c.* 1490.

　　trone throne

"Dere Sone," she seyde, "The Kyng of Blisse,
  That is so heighe in trone,
Knoweth that Thou didest nevere amys—
24   Why sholdest thou deye allone?"

"Moder," He seyde, "only of thee
  I took bothe flessh and bon
To save mankynde and make it free
28   Wyth myn herte blood allone."

"Dere Sone," she seyde, "Thou art equal
  To God, that is in trone;
For man, ther-fore, that is so thral,
32   Why sholdest Thou deye allone?"

"Moder," He seyde, "my Faders wylle
  And myn they ben but oon;
Ther-fore by skile I moot fulfille
36   My Faders wylle allone."

"Dere Sone," she seyde, "sith Thou hast take
  Of me bothe flessh and bon,
If it may be, me not forsak
40   In care and wo allone."

"For man I moot the raunsoun paye,
  The which to helle is gon,
"Moder," He seyde, "on Good Friday,
44   For he may not allone."

"Dere Sone," she seyde unto Him tho,
  "Whan Thou from me art gon,
Than shal I lyve in care and wo
48   Wythoute confort allone."

31. thral enslaved
35. skile reason

156

"Moder," He seyde, "tak thou no thoght—
　　For me make thou no mone;
Whan I have boght that I have wroght
52　　Thou shalt not be allone.

"On the thridde day, I thee bihighte,
　　After that I am gon,
I wol arise by my grete myght
56　　And conforte thee allone."

49. *thoght* for MS. *nought*
53. **bihighte** promise

90

Sancta Maria, ora pro nobis.

O Moder mylde, Mayde undefiled,
That we so wilde be not bigiled
   And evere exiled from Crist and his,
4   *Ora pro nobis.*

O Quene of grace, moste faire of face,
Of al solas ledying the trace,
   Of that heighe place that we not mysse,
8   *Ora pro nobis.*

O Lady free, of heighe degree,
That we mowen see thy Sone and thee
   And evere to be wher al joye is,
12   *Ora pro nobis.*

That Crist us sende grace to amende
Oure tyme myspent er we hennes wende,
   And at oure ende to graunte us blisse,
16   *Ora pro nobis.*

Index 2527. Camb. Univ. MS. Ee. 1. 12. (*EEC* No. 220.)
Unique text. By James Ryman. *c.* 1490.

   Sancta Maria, ora pro nobis Saint Mary, pray for us
 2. **wilde** wayward, unsubmitting
 6. **ledyng the trace** at the forefront of a line or procession, i.e., excelling,
   exceeding
14. **hennes wende** turn (go), hence, i.e., die

91

Revert, revert, revert, revert!
O synful man, yif me thyn herte.

Have mynde how I mankynde have take
Of a pure mayde, man, for thy sake,
That were most bounde most free to make.
4   O synful man, yif me thyn herte.

Have mynde, thou synful creature,
I took baptesme in thy nature
From filthe of synne to make thee pure.
8   O synful man, yif me thyn herte.

Mave mynde, man, how I took the feeld,
Upon my bak berying my sheeld;
For peyne ne deeth I wolde not yelde.
12   O synful man, yif me thyn herte.

Have mynde, I was put on the rode
And for thy sake shedde myn herte blood;
Bihold my peyne—biholde my mood!
16   O synful man, yif me thyn herte.

Bihold me, hed, hond, foot, and side!
Bihold my woundes five so wide!
Bihold the peyne that I abide!
20   O synful man, yif me thyn herte.

Index 1125. Camb. Univ. MS. Ee. 1. 12. (*EEC* No. 269.)
Unique text. By James Ryman. *c.* 1490.

1. **mankynde** i.e., human form

Have mynde, man, how faste I was bounde
For thy sake to a piler rounde,
Scourged til my blood fil to grounde.
24   O synful man, yif me thyn herte.

Have mynde how I in forme of breed
Have left my flessh and blood to wedde
To make thee quik whan thou art deed.
28   O synful man, yif me thyn herte.

Have mynde, man, how I have thee wroght,
How wyth my blood I have thee boght,
And how to blisse I have thee broght.
32   O synful man, yif me thyn herte.

O synful man, bihold and see
What I have don and do for thee
If thou wylt be in blisse wyth me.
36   O synful man, yif me thyn herte.

Bothe for my deeth and peynes smerte
That I suffred for thy desserte
I axe namore, man, but thyn herte:
40   Revert, revert, revert, revert.

22. **rounde** (?) openly, without concealment
26. **to wedde** as a pledge
38. **desserte** desert, i.e., what is deserved

92

O man unkynde,
Have thou in mynde
My passioun smerte!
4 Thou shalt me fynde
To thee ful kynde:
Lo, heer myn herte.

Index 2507. Trinity Coll. Camb. MS. 1157. (Henry A. Person, *Cambridge Middle English Lyrics*, 2d ed., No. 9.)
Two other texts. Fifteenth century.

93

Ther bloweth a cold wynd to-day, to-day,
The wynd bloweth cold to-day;
Crist suffred his passioun for mannes salvacioun
To kepe the colde wynd awey.

This wynd by resoun is called temptacioun—
    It raveth bothe nyght and day;
Remembre, man, how thy Saveour was slawen
4   To kepe the colde wynd awey.

Pride and presumpcioun and fals extorcioun
    That many man don bitraye—
Man, com to contricioun and axe confessioun
8   To kepe the colde wynd awey.

O Mary mylde, for love of thy child
    That deyde on Good Friday,
Be oure salvacioun from mortal dampnacioun
12   To kepe the colde wynd awey.

He was nayled, his blood was haled,
    Oure remissioun for-to beye,
And for oure synnes alle He drank bothe eisel and galle
16   To kepe the colde wynd awey.

Index 3525. MS. Ashmole 1379 [= Bodl. 7683]. (*EEC* No. 170.)
Unique text. *c.* 1500.

9. *thy* for MS. *the*
13. **haled** caused to flow (in a large stream)
15. **eisel** vinegar

Slouthe, envye, covetise, and lechery
    Blewe the colde wynd, as I dar seye;
Ayeins swich poyson He suffred his passioun
20   To kepe the colde wynd awey.

O man, remembre the Lord so tendre
    Which deyde wythouten denay;
His hondes so smerte laye next to his herte
24   To kepe the colde wynd awey.

Now preye we alle to the kyng celestial,
    That born He was of may,
That we mowen love so wyth othere mo
28   To kepe the colde wynd awey.

At the day of doom whan we shullen come
    Oure synnes not for-to denaye,
Mary, preye to thy Sone that sightly is in trone
32   To kepe the colde wynd awey.

At the laste ende, man, thou shalt sende
    And kepe bothe nyght and day;
The moste goodliest tresour is Crist the Saveour
36   To kepe the colde wynd awey.

Heer lat us ende, and Crist us defende
    Al by the nyght and by day,
And brynge us to his place where is myrthe and solas
40   To kepe the colde wynd awey.

31. **trone** throne; *thy* for MS. *the* and *is in* for MS. *yn hys*
37. **Crist** for MS. *agenyst*

Allone, allone, allone, allone, allone—
Heer I sitte allone, alas! allone.

As I walked me this endre day
To the grene-wode for-to pleye
And al hevynesse to putte awey,
4   My-self allone;—

As I walked under the grene-wode bough
I saw a mayde faire ynough;
A child she happed, she song, she lough,—
8   That child wepede allone.

"Sone," she seyde, "I have Thee born
To save mankynde that was forlorn;
There-fore I preye Thee, Sone, ne murne,
12   But be stille allone."

"Moder, me thinketh it is right ille
That men me sechen for-to spille,
For hem to save it is my wylle;
16   Ther-fore I cam hider allone."

"Sone," she seyde, "lat it be in thy thoght,
For mannes gilt is not wyth-soght;
For Thou art He that hath al wroght,
20   And I thy moder allone."

Index 364. B.M. Addit. MS. 5465. (*RL XV* No. 2.)
With music. Unique text. *c.* 1500.

7. **happed** clasped, protected; **lough** laughed
14. **spille** destroy, kill; *me* not in MS.
18. **wyth-soght** pursued; *soght* for MS. *stone*

95

Who wot now that is heer
Wher he shal be another yeer?

Another yeer it may bitide
This companye to ben ful wide,
And nevere another heer to abide—
4   Crist may sende now swich a yeer.

Another yeer it may bifalle
The leste that is wythinne this halle
To ben more maister thanne we alle—
8   Crist may sende now swich a yeer.

Thise lordes that ben wonder grete,
They threten poure men for-to bete;
It lendeth litel in her threte—
12   Crist may sende now swich a yeer.

Index 320. B.M. Addit. MS. 40166(C3). (*EEC* No. 121.)
Unique text. Fifteenth century.

6. **The leste** the least, the lowliest (one)
11. **It lendeth litel** little dwells, is contained
12. *now* not in MS.

Hey, ey, hey, ey,
Make we myrie as we may.

Now is Yole comen wyth gentil chere—
Of myrthe and gamen he hath no pere;
In every lond wher he cometh nere
4   Is myrthe and gamen, I dar wel seye.

Now is comen a messager
Of thy lord, Sir Newe Yeer;
Biddeth us alle ben myrie heer
8   And make as myrie as we may.

Ther-fore every man that is heer
Synge a carole on his manere;
If he can non we shullen him lere,
12   So that we ben myrie alwey.

Whose-evere maketh hevy chere,
Were he nevere to me dere,
In a dich I wolde he were
16   To drye his clothes til it were day.

Mende the fyr and make good chere!
Fill the cuppe, sire boteler!
Lat every man drynke to his fere!
20   This endeth my carole wyth care awey.

Index 2343. B.M. Addit. MS. 14997. (*SL XIV-XV* No. 3.)
Unique text. October 4, 1500.

  1. **Yole** Yuletide
13. **maketh hevy chere** is somber, causes unhappiness
19. **fere** fellow, companion

97

Bon jour, bon jour a vous!
I am come unto this hous,
  Wyth par la pompe, I seye.

Is ther any good man heer
That wyl make me any chere?
And if ther were 1 wolde come nere
4   To wite what he wolde seye.
    A! Wol ye ben wilde?
    By Mary mylde,

      . . . . .

8   I trowe ye wol synge gaye.

Beth gladly, maistres, everichoon!
I am come my-self allone
To appose you oon by oon.
12   Lat see who dar seye nay.—
    Sire, what seye ye?
    Syng on, lete us see.—
    Now wyl it be
16   This or another day?

Index 1609. Balliol Coll. Oxf. MS. 354. (*SL XIV-XV* No. 1.)
Unique text. *c.* 1500.

  par la pompe with ceremonial celebration, procession
 5. **wilde** wayward, uncooperative
11. **appose** interrogate, examine
13. **seye ye** here, and in following lines, the pronoun of address (i.e., second
    person) is plural in form, as a mark of respect, even though the referent
    is singular

Lo, this is he that wyl don the dede:
He trempreth his mouth—ther-fore tak hede—
Syng softe, I seye, lest youre nose blede,
20   For hurte your-self ye may.
           But by God that me boghte,
           Youre brest is so toght,
           Til ye have wel coughed
24   Ye may not ther-wyth awey.

Sire, what seye ye wyth youre face so lene?
Ye synge neither good tenour, treble, ne mene.
Utter not youre vois wythoute youre brest be clene,
28   Hertely I you preye.
           I holde you excused,
           Ye shal ben refused,
           For ye have not ben used
32   To no good sport ne pleye.

Sire, what seye ye wyth youre fat face?
Me thinketh ye sholde beren a very good base
To a pot of good ale or ypocras,
36   Trewely as I you seye!
           Hold up youre hed,
           Ye loke like leed;
           Ye waste muche breed
40   Evermore from day to day.

18. **trempreth** makes ready
20. **thou may** = *thou mayst*
22. **toght** taut, pressed tight; congested
35. **ypocras** spiced wine, a cordial

Now wol ye see wher he stondeth bihynde?
Y-wis, brother, ye ben unkynde!
Stond forth and waste wyth me som wynd,
44   For ye have been called a synger ay.
       Nay, be not ashamed,
       Ye shal not ben blamed,
       For ye have been famed
48   The worst in this contree!

98

Make we myrie bothe more and lasse
For now is the tyme of Cristemasse.

Lat no man come into this halle—
Grome, page, nor yet marchal—
But that some sport he brynge wyth-al,
4   For now is the tyme of Cristemasse.

If that he seye he can noght synge,
Som other sport than lat him brynge
That it may plese at this festeyinge,
8   For now is the tyme of Cristemasse.

If he seye he can noght do,
Than for my love axe him no mo,
But to the stokkes than lat him go,
12   For now is the tyme of Cristemasse.

Index 1866. Balliol Coll. Oxf. MS. 354. (*SL XIV-XV* No. 2.)
Unique text. *c.* 1500.

lasse = *lesse*
2. **marchal** marshal (for ceremonial occasion)
3. **sport** amusement, entertainment (disport)
7. **festeyinge** feasting

99

Lullay, lullay, lully, lullay,
The faucon hath born my make awey.

He bar him up, he bar him down,
He bar him into an orchard broun.

In that orchard ther was an halle
4   That was hanged wyth purpre and palle.

And in that halle there was a bed,
It was hanged wyth gold so red.

And in that bed ther lieth a knight,
8   His woundes bledyng day and nyght.

By that beddes side ther kneleth a may,
And she wepeth bothe nyght and day.

And by that beddes side ther stondeth a ston,
12   *Corpus Cristi* writen ther-on.

Index 1132. Balliol Coll. Oxf. MS. 354. (*EEC* No. 322A.)
Three traditional versions recorded in nineteenth century. *c.* 1500.

faucon falcon
1. **bar him** is a reflexive construction: he went, flew
4. **purpre and palle** rich and fine (purple) cloth

100

For wele or wo I wyl not flee
To love that herte that loveth me.

That herte myn herte hath in swich grace
   That of two hertes oon herte make we;
That herte hath broght my herte in cas
4   To love that herte that loveth me.

For oon that like unto that herte
   Nevere was nor is nor nevere shal be,
Nor nevere like cause sette this aparte
8   To love that herte that loveth me;

Which cause yeveth cause to me and myn
   To serve that herte of soverayntee,
And stille to synge this lattere lyne:
12   To love that herte that loveth me.

What-evere I seye, what-evere I synge,
   What-evere I do, that herte shal see
That I shal serve wyth herte lovynge
16   That lovynge herte that loveth me.

This knotte thus knyt who shal untwyne,
   Sith wc that knytte it don agree
To lose ne slyppe, but bothe enclyne
20   To love that herte that loveth me?

Index 3271. Canterbury Cathedral: Christ Church Letters, Vol. II, No. 174. (*EEC* No. 444.)
Unique text. *c.* 1500.

Farewel, of hertes that herte most fyn,
　Farewel, dere herte, hertely to thee,
And kepe this herte of myn for thyn
24　　As herte for herte for lovyng me.

SELECTED FRAGMENTS

Swete lemman, thyn ore!

(LLME, p. 161)

At the wrastlyng my lemman I ches, [chose]
And at the ston-castyng I him for-les. [lost]

(LLME, p. 162)

Dore, go thou stille,
Go thou stille, stille,
That I have in the boure
I-don al my wylle, wylle.

(LLME, p. 167)

Ge[yn]eth me no gerlond of grene [is worthy of me]
But it be of withins i-wroght. [willow branches]

(LLME, p. 182)

Com hider, love, to me!

(LLME, p. 183)

I have loved so many a day,
Lightly sped, but bettre I may.

This endre day whan me was wo
Nyghtengale to move me to
Under a bough ther I lay. . . .

(LLME, p. 171)

Brid on brere I telle it to—
Non other I ne dar.

(LLME, p. 171)

God graunte me grace to gete ageyn
The love that I have lost.

(LLME, p. 172)

I come hider to wowe. . . .

(LLME, p. 184)

The ship saileth over the salte fom
Wyl brynge her marchantz and my lemman hom.

(LLME, p. 184)

Princesse of youthe and flour of godlihede,
The parfite mirour of al gentilesse.

(LLME, p. 185)

My love she murneth for me, for me,
My love she murneth for me.

(LLME, p. 172)

Amonges alle myrthes many
We shullen synge of oon lady—
In al this world nis swich a sight.

(LLME, p. 175)

I am not unkynde
To love as I fynde. . . .

(LLME, p. 172)

She speketh noght ne sheweth forth hir face
To me that longe hath waited for hir grace. . . .

(Untraced)

Lie thou me neer, lemman,
In thyne armes. . . .

(LLME, p. 172)

SELECTED BIBLIOGRAPHY

A. PRINCIPAL COLLECTIONS

Brook, G. L., ed. *The Harley Lyrics*. 2d ed. Manchester, 1956.
Brown, Carleton, ed. *English Lyrics of the XIIIth Century*. Oxford, 1932.
——, ed. *Religious Lyrics of the XIVth Century*. 2d ed., revised by G. V. Smithers. Oxford, 1957.
——, ed. *Religious Lyrics of the XVth Century*. Oxford, 1939.
Greene, Richard Leighton, ed. *The Early English Carols*. Oxford, 1935. 2d ed., revised and enlarged, Oxford, 1977.
——, ed. *A Selection of English Carols*. Oxford, 1962.
Person, Henry, ed. *Cambridge Middle English Lyrics*. Revised ed. Seattle, 1962.
Robbins, Rossell Hope, ed. *Secular Lyrics of the Fourteenth and Fifteenth Centuries*. Oxford, 1952.
——, ed. *Historical Poems of the Fourteenth and Fifteenth Centuries*. Oxford, 1959.

B. OTHER COLLECTIONS AND EDITIONS

Chambers, E. K., and F. Sidgwick, eds. *Early English Lyrics*. London, 1907.
Davies, R. T., ed. *Medieval English Lyrics*. London, 1963.
Dickins, Bruce, and R. M. Wilson, eds. *Early Middle English Texts*. London, 1951.
Dobson, E. J., and F. Ll. Harrison, eds. *Medieval English Songs*. London, 1979.
Gray, Douglas, ed. *A Selection of Religious Lyrics*. Oxford, 1975.
Ker, N. R., ed. *Facsimile of British Museum MS. Harley 2253*. Early English Text Society, 255. London, 1965.
Loomis, R. S., and R. Willard, *Medieval English Verse and Prose in Modernized Versions*. New York, 1948.
Luria, M. S., and R. L. Hoffman, eds. *Middle English Lyrics*. New York, 1965.

Morris, Richard, ed. *An Old English Miscellany.* Early English Text Society, o. s. 49. London, 1872.

Silverstein, T., ed. *Medieval English Lyrics.* London, 1971.

Stemmler, T., ed. *Medieval English Love-Lyrics.* Tübingen, 1970.

C. Reference Materials

Dictionaries and Glossaries:

The Oxford English Dictionary. J. A. H. Murray et al., eds. Oxford, 1884–1928; corrected re-issue, 1933.

Middle English Dictionary. H. Kurath, S. M. Kuhn, and Robert Lewis, eds. Ann Arbor, 1952–.

Davis, Norman. "Glossary," for *Early Middle English Verse and Prose*, ed. J. A. W. Bennett and G. V. Smithers. Oxford, 1968. (Includes a selection of twenty-three lyrics.)

Davis, N. et al., eds. *A Chaucer Glossary.* Oxford, 1979.

Stratmann, F. H., ed. *A Middle-English Dictionary.* Revised and enlarged by H. Bradley. Oxford, 1891.

Tolkien, J. R. R. "A Middle English Vocabulary," in *Fourteenth-Century Verse and Prose*, ed. Kenneth Sisam. Oxford, 1921. (Includes a selection of nine lyrics.)

Other Textual and Linguistic References:

Blake, Norman, ed. *The Cambridge History of the English Language*, Vol. 2, 1066–1476. Cambridge, 1992.

Brown, Carleton, and Rossell Hope Robbins. *The Index of Middle English Verse.* New York, 1943.

Jordan, Richard. *Handbuch der mittelenglischen Grammatick.* Heidelberg, 1925. Trans. E. J. Crook as *Handbook of Middle English Grammar.* The Hague, 1974.

Mossé, Fernand. *Manuel de l'anglais du moyen age.* Paris, 1949. Trans. James A. Walker as *A Handbook of Middle English.* Baltimore, 1952. (Includes glossary, grammar and a selection of six lyrics.)

Mustanoja, Tauno. *A Middle English Syntax: Part I.* Helsinki, 1960.

Preston, Michael J. A. *A Concordance to the Middle English Shorter Poem.* 2 vols. Leeds, 1975.

Robbins, Rossell Hope, and John Levi Cutler. *Supplement to the Index of Middle English Verse.* Lexington, Ky., 1965.

Wilson, E. A. *A Descriptive Catalogue of the English Lyrics in John of Grimestone's Preaching Book.* Medium Aevum Monographs, n. s. 2. Oxford, 1973.

Wilson, R. M. *The Lost Literature of Medieval England.* London, 1952.

D. SCHOLARSHIP AND CRITICISM

Allen, Judson Boyce. "Grammar, Poetic Form, and the Lyric Ego: A Medieval a priori." In Ebin, pp. 199–226.

Barratt, Alexandra. "The Prymer and Its Influence on Fifteenth-Century Passion Lyrics." *Medium Aevum* 44 (1975), 264–79.

Bolton, W. F. "The Conditions of Literary Composition in Medieval England." In Bolton, pp. 1-27.

———. ed. *The Middle Ages.* Vol. 1 of *History of Literature in the English Language.* New York, 1987.

Bowra, Maurice. *Medieval Love-Song.* London, 1961.

Chambers, E. K. "Some Aspects of Medieval Lyric." In *Early English Lyrics,* ed. Chambers and F. Sidgwick (see section B).

———. "The Carol and Fifteenth-Century Lyric." In Chambers, *English Literature at the Close of the Middle Ages,* pp. 66–121. Oxford, 1945.

Curtius, Ernst Robert. *Europäische Literatur und lateinisches Mittelalter.* Bern, 1948. Trans. Willard Trask as *European Literature and the Latin Middle Ages.* Bollingen Series 36. Princeton, 1953.

Diehl, Patrick S. *The Medieval European Religious Lyric.* Berkeley, 1985.

Dronke, Peter. *Medieval Latin and the Rise of European Love-Lyric.* 2 vols. Oxford, 1965–66.

———. *The Medieval Lyric.* London, 1968.

Ebin, Lois. "Poetics and Style in Late Medieval Literature." In Ebin, pp. 263–93.

———, ed. *Vernacular Poetics in the Middle Ages.* Kalamazoo, 1984.

Friedlander, Carolyn Van Dyke. "Early Middle English Accented Verse." *Modern Philology* 76 (1979), 219–30.

Gibinska, Marta. "The Early Middle English Lyrics as Compared to the Provençal and Latin Lyrics." *Kwartlanik Neofilologiczny,* 1974, 459–76.

———. "Some Observations on the Themes and Techniques of Medieval English Religious Lyrics." *English Studies* 57 (1976), 103–14.

Gray, Douglas. *Themes and Images in the Medieval Religious Lyric.* London, 1972.

———. "Lyrics." In J. A. W. Bennett, *Middle English Literature,* edited and completed by Douglas Gray, pp. 364–406. Oxford, 1986.

———. "Later Poetry: The Courtly Tradition." In Bolton, pp. 313–67.

Greene, Richard Leighton. "Carols." In *A Manual of Writings in Middle English 1050–1500,* vol. 6, ed. Albert E. Hartung, pp. 1753–808 and 2019–70 (bibliography). Hamden, Conn., 1980.

Hanson-Smith, Elizabeth. "A Woman's View of Courtly Love: The Findern Anthology Cambridge University Library MS. Ff. 1.6." *Journal of Women's Studies in Literature* 1 (1979), 179–94.

Howell, Andrew J. "Reading the Harley Lyrics: A Master Poet and the Language of Conventions." *ELH* 47 (1980), 619–45.

Jeffrey, David L. *The Early English Lyric and Franciscan Spirituality.* Lincoln, Neb., 1975.

Kane, George. *Middle English Literature: A Critical Study of the Romances, the Religious Lyrics, Piers Plowman.* Part 2. London, 1951.

———. "A Short Essay on the Middle English Secular Lyric." In *Studies Presented to Tauno F. Mustanoja on the Occasion of His Sixtieth Birthday. Neuphilologische Mitteilungen* 73.1–2 (1972), 110-21.

Lewis, C. S. *The Allegory of Love: A Study in Medieval Tradition.* Oxford, 1936.

———. *The Discarded Image: An Introduction to Medieval and Renaissance Literature.* Cambridge, 1964.

Manning, Stephen. *Wisdom and Number: Toward a Critical Appraisal of the Middle English Religious Lyric.* Lincoln, Neb., 1962.

Moore, Arthur K. *The Secular Lyric in Middle English.* Lexington, Ky., 1951.

Oliver, Raymond. *Poems without Names, the English Lyric 1200-1500.* Berkeley, 1970.

Olson, Glending. "Toward a Poetics of the Late Medieval Court Lyric." In Ebin, pp. 227–48.

Osberg, Richard H. "The Alliterative Lyric and Thirteenth-Century Devotional Prose." *Journal of English and Germanic Philology* 76 (1977), 40–54.

Pearsall, Derek. *Old English and Middle English Poetry.* London, 1977.

Plummer, John F., III. "The Poetic Function of Conventional Language In the Middle English Lyric." *Studies in Philology* 72 (1975), 367–85.

Raby, F. J. E. *A History of Christian-Latin Poetry from the Beginnings to the Close of the Middle Ages.* Oxford, 1927.

————. *A History of Secular Latin Poetry in the Middle Ages.* 2 vols. Oxford, 1934.

Ransom, Daniel. *Poets at Play: Irony and Parody in the Harley Lyrics.* Norman, Okla., 1985.

Reiss, Edmund. "A Critical Approach to the Middle English Lyric." *College English* 27 (1965–66), 373–79.

————. *The Art of the Middle English Lyric.* Athens, Georgia, 1972.

————. "Religious Commonplaces and Poetic Artistry in the Middle English Lyric." *Style* 4 (1976), 97–106.

Robbins, Rossell Hope. "Poems Dealing with Contemporary Conditions." In *A Manual of Writings in Middle English 1050-1500,* vol. 5, ed. Albert E. Hartung, pp. 1432–36 and 1631–1725 (bibliography). Hamden, Conn., 1975.

————. "The Middle English Court Love Lyric." In *The Interpretation of Medieval Lyric Poetry,* ed. W. T. H. Jackson, 205–32. New York, 1980.

Schofield, W. H. *English Literature from the Norman Conquest to Chaucer.* London, 1906.

Speirs, John. "Carols and Other Songs and Lyrics." In Speirs, *Medieval English Poetry: The Non-Chaucerian Tradition,* pp. 45–96. London, 1957.

Spitzer, Leo. "Explication de Texte Applied to Three Great Middle English Poems." *Archivum Linguisticum* 3 (1951), 1–22, 137–65. (A study of "Ichot a burde in boure bright," "I sing of a maiden," and "Lestenyt, Lordynges, both elde and yinge.")

Stevick, R. D. "The Criticism of Middle English Lyrics." *Modern Philology* 64 (1966), 103–17.

Stevens, Martin. "The Royal Stanza in Early English Literature." *PMLA* 94 (1979), 62–76.

Weber, Sarah A. *Theology and Poetry in the Middle English Lyric: A Study of Sacred History and Aesthetic Form.* Columbus, Ohio, 1969.

Wenzel, Siegfried. *Preacher, Poet, and the Early English Lyric.* Princeton, 1986.

Wilhelm, J. J. *The Cruelest Month: Spring, Nature, and Love in Classical and Medieval Lyrics.* New Haven, Conn., 1965.

Woolf, Rosemary. *The English Religious Lyric in the Middle Ages.* Oxford, 1968.

———. "Later Poetry: The Popular Tradition." In Bolton, pp. 267–311.

GLOSSARY

Words glossed on the same page on which they occur in the poems are not listed below, unless (1) they have been assigned specialized meanings in specific texts but occur elsewhere with more usual meanings; or (2) it is convenient to list the inflectional forms in one place, here in the Glossary. (See Introduction, pp. xvii–xviii.)

Inflectional forms of nouns, adjectives, and verbs are given as needed. Two forms of verbs in parentheses following the headword are preterite singular and passive participle; three such forms are preterite singular, preterite plural, and passive participle.

aboute (adv., prep.) about, around

adrede(n) fear, be afraid

afore, aforn before, beforehand, formerly

al (adj. and noun) pl. **alle** all, every; everything

al (adv.) entirely, very, quite, wholly

also (adv.) also, equally, similarly; **as** (conj.) as, as if
   also soon as soon as

amende(n) to make better, improve, make amends, set right

axe(n) ask, inquire; require

ay always, ever, continually, on every occasion

ayeins against

bad *see* **bidde(n)**

bale torment, misery, misfortune, sorrow

bar *see* **bere(n)**

be(n) to be Pr. sg. 1 **am**, 2 **art, best**, 3 **is, beth**; pl. **ben, beth**; subj. sg. **be**, pl. **ben**. Pt. sg. 1, 3 **was**, 2 **were, wast**; pl. **were(n)**; subj. sg. **were**, pl. **were(n)**. Ppl. **ben, i-be**. Imp. sg. **be**, pl. **beth**

bere(n) (**bar, beren, born**) to bear, carry, possess, hold; give birth to

best best. *See also* **be(n)**

beste beast, animal, creature

bete(n) (**bette, bete(n)**) to beat, scourge

beye(n) (**boghte, boght**) to buy, pay for, redeem

bidde(n) (**bad, bidden**) to pray, ask, bid; offer; command

bifore, biforn before

bihete(n) (**bihete, bihote**) to promise

biknowe(n) to acknowledge, confess; recognize

bileve (noun) belief, faith

bille letter, note

biseche(n) (**bisoghte, bisoght**) to beseech, entreat, implore

bisee(n) to attend to, heed

bisynesse activity; preoccupation; care, anxiety

bithenke(n) (bithoghte, bithoght) to reflect, bethink, consider, concern oneself

bitide(n) to happen, befall

blisse happiness, bliss, joy

blithe happy, glad, blithe

blosme blossom, flower

blynne(n) to cease, cease from

bon bone

boon boon, request, prayer

bour abode, chamber, dwelling-place, bower

breed bread

breke(n) (brak, breken, broken) to break

brenne(n) to burn

brid (young) bird

burde maiden

but but; unless; except

can (pr. pl. **conne**) to know, understand; be able, know how to, can

cas circumstance, case; affair; condition, plight

chere face, appearance, demeanor; (good) cheer

clene clean, pure; splendid; **clennesse** cleanness, purity

clepe(n) to call, name, summon; mention

come(n) (cam, comen, comen) to come

conne *see* **can**

cosse kiss

dar (inf. **durre(n)**, pt. **durste**) to dare

dayesyes daisies

debonaire, deboner gracious, courteous; of good disposition

dede deed, event, act

deed (adj., noun) pl. **dede** dead

deeth death

dele(n) to deal, allot, distribute, deal with, perform

demened (ppl. adj.) conducted, managed, expressed

dere (adj.) dear, beloved, valued; (adv.) dearly

deye(n) to die

disese discomfort, misery, sorrow, distress

do(n) to do, cause, act, make. Also as preterite auxiliary form. **do(n) wey** set aside, do away with, abolish

domes-day the Day of Judgment

doom judgment, decision

drawe(n) (drough, drawen) to draw, pull; bring; add

drede fear

drough *see* **drawe(n)**

ech each; **ech a** every

eke also, moreover

endite(n) to write, dictate or compose (for writing)

endre recent, just passed **endre day** a day or two ago

er (comp. **erre**) before, earlier, formerly. Also **er-than, er-that**

ete(n) (eet, eten, eten) to eat

everich (a) every

everichoon everyone

everydel altogether, every bit, in every part

eye pl. **eyen** eye

falle(n) (fil, fallen) to fall

fame fame, reputation; rumor; report

fare(n) (for, foren, faren) to go, fare, behave, conduct

faute fault

fautles faultless

fay, fey faith

fayn glad; eager, willing. Also adverb

feend pl. **fendes** devil; the Devil; foe

fer far

fey *see* **fay**

feyne(n) to feign, pretend

fil *see* **falle(n)**

flood pl. **flodes** flood, water, stream, sea

flour flower

fode food, sustenance

fond *see* **fynde(n)**

for for. *See also* **fare(n)**

forlete(n) to relinquish, give up entirely. *See also* **lete(n)**

forlorn (ppl. and adj.) lost; ruined, degraded

for-than because

for-thy therefore; because

founde(n) *see* **fynde(n)**

fowel bird, foul

free noble, gracious, generous; free; forward, immodest

fro from

fynde(n) (**fond, founde(n), founden**) to find

fyr fire

game, gamen amusement; game, sport; merriment; joy, pleasure

gan (pt. of **gynne**) began, undertook (and carried out). Also a verb auxiliary indicating past time: did

gest guest

gilt guilt

glee pl. **glewes** mirth, pleasure; entertainment; music

go(n) to go, walk, move. Pr. sg. 1 **go**, 2 **gost**, 3 **goth**; pl. **go(n)**; subj. sg. **go**, pl. **go(n)**. Pt. **went**. Ppl. **gon, i-go**. Imp. sg. **go**, pl. **goth**

gostly spiritual

grete(n) (pt. sg. 1, 3 **grette**) to greet

ground bottom, ground, base, foundation

gynne *see* **gan**

han *see* **have(n)**

hap chance, (good) fortune

have(n), han to have, possess, keep. Pr. sg. 1 **have**, 2 **havest, hast**, 3 **haveth, hath**; subj. sg. **have**, pl. **have(n)**. Pt. sg. 1, 3 **hadde**, 2 **haddest**, pl. **hadde(n)**. Ppl. **had, i-had**. Imp. sg. **have**, pl. **haveth**

hed head

heer (1) here; (2) pl. **heres** hair

heighe (adj., noun) high, noble. Also adverb

hele health; prosperity; recovery, restoration

hele(n) to heal, restore

hende (adj., noun) gracious courteous, gentle; pleasant

hennes hence

hente(n) to seize, obtain

herber arbor, garden, grassy place among trees

herbere(n) to harbor, protect

here(n) to hear, listen to

herie(n) to praise, worship; honor

herte heart

hevy heavy; sad

hewe hue, complexion, appearance, beauty

hond hand

ilke each every; **that ilke** that same, that very (one)

kene bold, eager, keen; sharp; cruel

kepe(n) to keep, preserve, take care of

kyn, kynne kin, race, kind

kynde (noun) nature; (adj.) kind; natural

ladden *see* lede(n)

largesse generosity, liberality

lat *see* lete(n)

leche physician; means of recovery

lede(n) (**ledde, ladden, led/i-lad**) to lead, guide; direct, bring

leef (noun) pl. **leves** leaf; (adj.) inflected **leve** dear, beloved

  leefly dear, lovely

lemman beloved (one); lover, sweetheart

lenger (comp. of **longe**) longer

lere(n) to learn; teach

lese(n) (ppl. **i-lorn**) to lose

lete(n) (**lett, letten**) to let, allow, permit; leave, relinquish, let go; abandon, forsake. Also **lat** as auxiliary for horatative mood

leve(n) to leave; abandon, neglect, forsake

leves *see* **leef**

light (noun, adj.) light

like(n) to please. Also in impersonal constructions: e.g., **thee liketh** it pleases you

  like ille to displease

likne(n) to liken, compare

liste(n) as impersonal verb, to desire, wish; be pleased; e.g., **thee list** it pleases you; **me listeth** it pleases me

lite, litel little, small

lore instruction; doctrine

(i-)lorn *see* lese(n)

loude loudly

lufsom (comp. **lufsomer**) lovesome; beautiful, lovely

lust pleasure, desire, delight; lust

lusty desirable, pleasant

make mate

  makeles without mate, matchless, peerless

mankynde, mankynne mankind

may (1) maiden; (2) pr. pl. **mowe(n)** may, can, be able, be permitted

mede reward, meed; bribe

meed (1) meadow; (2) mead (a fermented drink)

mele meal, repast

mete food

mo more

moder mother

mone (1) complaint, lamentation, moan; (2) moon

mood mood, spirit, temper; thought; mind

moot (pr. sg. 1, 3 **moot**, 2 **most**, pl. **mote(n)**; pt. **moste**) must; can; may

morwe morning, morrow; day

morwenynge morning

mowe *see* **may** (2)

muche, muchel much, great. Also adverb

murier, muriest *see* **myrie**

murne(n) to mourn, lament, sorrow

myddel middle; waist

myrie (murier, muriest) merry, gay, joyous, pleasant. Also adverb

myrthe joy, mirth; amusement; pleasure

myschief misfortune, distress, adversity

mysese discomfort; trouble, harm

namore (adj.) = *no more* no other, nothing more; (adv.) nevermore

ne a negative particle

neer *see* **nere**

neighe(n) to approach, near

nemne(n) to name, mention

nere (comp. **neer**) near

nis = *ne is*

noght (noun) nothing (at all); (adv.) not, not at all

nyl = *ne wyl*

o, oo ever, always

of of; from; out of

oon (pronoun) one (person, thing, etc.); (adj.) one, a single
  at ones once, on one (single) occasion

oone (adv.) alone, only

ore favor; grace; mercy

oth oath

other (adj.) second; other; (noun) others; (conj.) or

owene, owe (adj.) own

parfit perfect

pere equal, peer

peyne pain, distress, torment, suffering

pleye(n) to play, amuse oneself

pleying play, amusement, sport, entertainment

poure poor

preye(n) to pray; beseech

prike(n) to prick, cause to ache

pris worth, excellence; prize

prively privately, intimately

propre (adj.) own

pyne misery, torment, pain, grief

pyne(n) to (cause) torment, pain; cause misery, cause grief

ran *see* **renne(n)**

rede advice, counsel
  what shal me to rede what shall I do

rede(n) to advise, counsel

renne(n) (ran, ronne, ronne) to run, go; flow

reve(n) to bereave, take away; rob, plunder

rewe(n) to pity, have pity (for); rue, regret. Also impersonal verb, e.g., **me reweth** I have pity (or regret) for; **it reweth me** I regret, it causes me regret

reweful rueful, pitiable; sad, grievous

rode rood, cross

ronne *see* **renne(n)**

saw *see* **see(n)**

seche(n) (soghte, soght) to seek, search

see(n) (saw, sawen, seen) to see, perceive

seemly seemly, fair, becoming

sene manifest, visible

seur sure

seven-nyght seven nights; a week

seye(n), seyn to say; tell

shal (pr. pl. **shullen**) shall, will; am to (is to, etc.), ought to. Also as auxiliary verb

shene fair, shining, beautiful

shilde(n) to shield, protect; defend

shrynke(n) to wither, shrink

sik (1) (noun) sigh; (2) (adj.) sick

sike(n) to sigh; regret

siker (adj.) sure, certain, secure. Also as adverb

sith (adv. and conj.) afterward, after (that); since, after, when;
  sithen afterward;
  sith-that from the time that

slawen *see* **slee(n)**

slee(n) (ppl. **slayn/slawen**) to slay, strike down

so so; as

soghte *see* **seche(n)**

solas solace, consolation; comfort

somer springtime

sone son

song song. *See also* **synge(n)**

sonne sun

sooth (noun) (the) truth; (adj.) true
  for sothe forsooth, in truth, truly

sore (noun) pain, sore, misery; (adj.) sore, grievous, painful; (adv.) sorely, grievously, painfully; exceedingly

sorwe sorrow, grief, pain

sorwe(n) to grieve, (cause) sorrow

speke(n) to speak, talk

spray (small) branch, spray

sprynge(n) (**sprong, sprongen**) to spring; sprout, grow

stal *see* **stele(n)**

stark strong, powerful; severe

stele(n) (**stal, stelen, stolen**) to steal

sterre star

stinge(n) (ppl. **stongen**) to pierce; sting

stolen *see* **stele(n)**

stonde(n) to stand; remain

stongen *see* **stinge(n)**

stounde space of time, short time; moment; time of suffering

stour strong, stalwart

stout strong; proud; stately, magnificent

stynte(n) to stint, cease, stop

sustene(n) to sustain

swete (**swetter, swettest**) (adj.) sweet; pleasant; (noun) sweet one

swetyng beloved, sweetheart, sweet one

swich such

swinge(n) (ppl. **swongen**) to strike, beat, whip

swithe very (much), exceedingly; quickly

synge(n) (**song, songen, songen**) to sing

synne sin

telle(n) to tell, recount; to count, enumerate

tente intent, notice

tere (noun) tear

than then, thereupon, afterward; consequently

thanne than

that (demonstrative pronoun) pl. **tho** that, pl. those; (relative pronoun) that

thenke(n) (**thoghte, thoght**) to think, conceive, consider

thennes thence

this pl. **thise** this, pl. these

tho then. *See also* **that**

thoghte *see* **thenke(n), thynke(n)**

thole(n) to endure, suffer; be patient

thrynge(n) to press, thrust, make (one's) way

thurgh through; by means of; because of

thyng pl. **thyng/thynges** thing; pl. things, affairs, matters

thynke(n) (**thoghte, thought**) impersonal verb, to seem (to)

tide time

togidre together

trowe(n) to believe, think

uncouth strange, foreign; unknown

under under, beneath; behind

variaunce inconstancy

wan pale, wan; dark

waxe(n) (**wex, wexen, waxen**) to wax, grow; become

wei woe

wel wel; many, much; easily; good; very

wele happiness, good fortune, wealth, prosperity

wende(n) to turn, change; go (away), depart; pass

wene(n) to expect; suppose, imagine; think

wepe(n) to weep

werke(n) (ppl. **wroght**) to work, cause, make, bring about

werre war

whan when

whil (conj.) while

while (noun) a time, while

whilom formerly, once

wight wight, person, creature

wit mind; judgment, understanding

wite(n) to know, learn; be aware, hold in mind. Pr. sg. 1, 3 **wot**, 2 **wost**; pl. **wiste**

wode wood, forest

wol, wollen *see* **wylle**

wone(n) to dwell, live; remain

wood mad

wot *see* **wite(n)**

wowe(n) to woo, make love

wroght *see* **werke(n)**

wrong (noun) wrong, injustice; (adj.) wrong, unjust

wronge (adv.) wrongfully, unjustly

wyth wronge wrongfully, unjustly

wroth angry

wyl, wylle will, desire; purpose

wylle to wish, desire, be willing. Also as auxiliary verb pr. sg. 1, 3 **wyl, wol,** 2 **wylt, wolt;** pl. **wol, wollen,** pt. sg. **wolde,** pl. 3 **wolde(n)**

wynne joy, bliss

wynne(n) to win, get, gain

yelde(n) to yield, produce; repay

yeve(n) (**yaf, yeven, yeven**) to give, grant

yift gift

yore a long time (ago), of old; since long ago; for long

yse ice

y-wis certainly, indeed, truly

Index of First Lines

First lines of refrains are indexed in italic.